THIS IS
OUR YOUTH

A PLAY BY KENNETH LONERGAN

THE OVERLOOK PRESS
NEW YORK, NY

First published in the United States in 2000 by
The Overlook Press, Peter Mayer Publishers, Inc.

NEW YORK:
141 Wooster Street
New York, NY 10012
www.overlookpress.com
For bulk and special sales, contact sales@overlookny.com,
or write us at the above address.

Cataloging-in-Publication Data is available from the Library of Congress

Book design and type formatting by Bernard Schleifer
Manufactured in the United States of America

9 8

ISBN: 978-1-4683-1107-5

CHARACTERS IN THE PLAY

DENNIS ZIEGLER, 21 years old
WARREN STRAUB, 19 years old
JESSICA GOLDMAN, 19 years old

✿ ✿ ✿ ✿ ✿

The play takes place in Dennis's one-room apartment
on the Upper West Side of Manhattan.

The time is late March, 1982.

*World Premiere originally presented by
The New Group:
Scott Elliott, Artistic Director;
Claudia Catania, Executive Producer*

PRODUCTION HISTORY

THIS IS OUR YOUTH was first produced by The New Group (Scott Elliott, Artistic Directory; Claudia Catania, Executive Producer), in New York City, in October, 1996. It was directed by Mark Brokaw. The cast was as follows:

DENNIS ZIEGLER	Josh Hamilton
WARREN STRAUB	Mark Ruffalo
JESSICA GOLDMAN	Missy Yager

THIS IS OUR YOUTH was produced by Second Stage Theatre (Carole Rothman, Artistic Director; Carol Fishman, Managing Director; Alexander Fraser, Executive Director), by special arrangement with Barry and Fran Weissler and The New Group (Scott Elliott, Artistic Directory; Claudia Catania, Executive Producer), in New York City, in November, 1998. It was directed by Mark Brokaw; the set design was by Allen Moyer; the costume design was by Michael Krass; the lighting design was by Mark McCullough; the sound design was by Robert Murphy; the fight director was Rick Sordeler; and the production stage manager was William H. Lang. The cast was as follows:

DENNIS ZIEGLER	Mark Rosenthal
WARREN STRAUB	Mark Ruffalo
JESSICA GOLDMAN	Missy Yager

THIS IS OUR YOUTH was produced by Steppenwolf Theatre Company (Martha Lavey, Artistic Director; David Hawkanson, Executive Director), at the Upstairs Theatre in Chicago, Illinois, in June, 2014. It was directed by Anna D. Shapiro; the set design was by Todd Rosenthal; the costume design was by Ann Roth; the lighting design was by Brian MacDevitt; the sound design was by Rob Milburn & Michael Bodeen; the fight director was Thomas Schall; and the production stage manager was Cambra Overend. The cast was as follows:

DENNIS ZIEGLER	Kieran Culkin
WARREN STRAUB	Michael Cera
JESSICA GOLDMAN	Tavi Gevinson

THIS IS OUR YOUTH was produced by Scott Rudin, Eli Bush, Roger Berlind, William Berlind, Jon B. Platt, Roy Furman, The Shubert Organization, Ruth Hendel, Scott M. Delman, Stephanie P. McClelland, Sonia Friedman, Tulchin Bartner, The Araca Group, Heni Koenigsberg, Daryl Roth, Joan Raffe & Jhett Tolentino, Catherine & Fred Adler and executive produced by Joey Parnes, Sue Wagner and John Johnson at the Cort Theatre in New York City in September 2014. It was directed by Anna D. Shapiro; the set design was by Todd Rosenthal; the costume design was by Ann Roth; the lighting design was by Brian MacDevitt; the sound design was by Rob Milburn & Michael Bodeen; the fight director was Thomas Schall; and the production stage manager was Cambra Overend. The cast was as follows:

DENNIS ZIEGLER	Kieran Culkin
WARREN STRAUB	Michael Cera
JESSICA GOLDMAN	Tavi Gevinson

ACT ONE

A cold Saturday night in March, 1982, after midnight. A small, imper-
sonal pillbox studio apartment on the second or third floor of a some-
what rundown postwar building on the Upper West Side of
Manhattan between Broadway and West End, lived in by DENNIS
ZIEGLER. *There are a TV and stereo, a lot of records, some arbitrary*
furniture, a little-used kitchenette, and a mattress on the floor in the
corner. Scattered around the room are piles of the New York Post,
sports magazines, and a lot of underground comic books. There is
sports equipment in the apartment, if not actually in view. The room
looks lived-in, but aside from a wall of photographs from DENNIS's *life,*
no effort whatsoever has been made to decorate it. It looks like it could
be packed up and cleared out in half an hour.

DENNIS *is watching an old black-and-white movie on TV. He is a*
grungy, handsome, very athletic, formerly long-haired kid, just
twenty-one years old, wearing baggy chino-type pants and an ancient
polo shirt. He is a very quick, dynamic, fanatical, and bullying kind of
person; amazingly good-natured and magnetic, but insanely competi-
tive and almost always successfully so; a dark cult god of high school
only recently encountering, without necessarily recognizing, the first
evidence that the dazzling, aggressive hipster techniques with which
he has always dominated his peers might not stand him in good stead
for much longer.

The buzzer buzzes. DENNIS *is too cool to answer it right away. It*
buzzes again. He gets up and goes to the intercom.

DENNIS

Yeah?

WARREN (*Over the intercom.*)

Yo, Dennis. It's me, Warren.

DENNIS

What do you want?

WARREN (*Over the intercom.*)

Yo, lemme up.

DENNIS *hits the buzzer. Sits down and watches TV. There is a knock at the door. Again, he doesn't answer it right away. Another knock.*

WARREN (*Off.*)

Yo, Denny.

DENNIS *gets up and unlocks the door without opening it, then plops down again to watch TV.*

WARREN STRAUB *comes in the front door. He is a skinny nineteen-year-old—an odd, kicked dog of a kid with large tracts of thoughtfulness in his personality that are not doing him much good at the moment, probably because they so infrequently influence his actions. He has spent most of his adolescence in hot water of one kind or another, but is just beginning to find beneath his natural eccentricity a dogged self-possession his friends may not all share. Despite his enormous self-destructiveness, he is above all things a trier, easily beaten back but hard to knock down. His language and wardrobe are heavily influenced by* DENNIS—*but only up to a point, and he would be a good-looking kid if he eased up on his personal style a little.*

He comes into the apartment lugging a very big suitcase and an over-loaded heavy-duty hiking backpack.

WARREN

Hey.

DENNIS

What's with the suitcase?

WARREN

Nothing . . . What are you doing?

DENNIS

Nothing.

WARREN *closes the door and puts down his stuff. Sits down next to* DENNIS *on the mattress and looks at the TV.*

WARREN

What are you watching?

DENNIS

Lock the door.

WARREN *gets up and locks the door. He sits down as before.*

WARREN

What are you watching?

DENNIS *flashes off the TV with the remote control.*

DENNIS

Nothing. What do you want?

WARREN

Nothing.

DENNIS

I don't have any pot.

WARREN

I don't want any. I got some.

DENNIS

Let me see it.

WARREN *produces a ziplock plastic bag carefully wrapped around a small amount of dark green marijuana.* DENNIS *opens it and smells it.*

DENNIS

This is good. Where'd you get it?

WARREN

From Christian.

DENNIS

Can we smoke it?

WARREN

I'm saving it.

DENNIS

For what?

DENNIS *takes the pot out of the bag and reaches for a record album. He starts to crumble the pot onto the album cover.*

WARREN

Just half.

DENNIS

Shut up.

WARREN

Just *half*, man.

DENNIS *looks at him and crumbles the rest of the pot onto the album.*

DENNIS

You got papers?

WARREN

You're a fuckin' asshole.

He gets up. DENNIS *laughs.*

DENNIS

There's some papers on the table. Gimme one.

WARREN *does not comply.*

DENNIS (*Sharply*)

Hey! Give me a *rolling* paper. Do you know how much *money* you owe me?

WARREN *takes out a small wad of bills, peels off a few, and drops them on the bed.*

DENNIS

Where'd you get this?

WARREN

What do you care?

DENNIS

Well if you're so rich then you can get more pot from Christian tomorrow, so give me the fucking rolling papers before I beat the shit out of you.

WARREN *goes to the table and throws a packet of Club or Zig-Zag rice papers to* DENNIS.

DENNIS

What happened, Jasonius kicked you out?

WARREN

No, man, I left.

DENNIS

You can't stay here.

WARREN

I don't want to stay here.

DENNIS

Why'd he kick you out? What'd you do?

WARREN

Nothing. I got stoned and he comes home and he's like, "This apartment smells like pot *all the time.*" And I'm like, "Yeah, 'cause I'm always *smoking* it." So then he's like, "I want that smell out of this house." And then he's like, "No, actually, I want *you* out of this house." Then he throws a few bills on the floor and is like, "There's some cash, now pack up your shit and get out before I beat your fuckin' head in." And I was like, "Whatever." So he went on a date with his whore, and I packed up my stuff and left.

DENNIS

Where are you going to stay?

WARREN

I don't know. Maybe I'll stay with Christian. I don't know.
Maybe I'll stay in a hotel. Who the hell knows?

DENNIS

How are you going to stay in a hotel?

WARREN

I got money.

DENNIS

How much did he give you?

WARREN

He gave me some money.

DENNIS

Why? Like to thank you for leaving?

WARREN

I guess.

DENNIS

How much is this?

Putting the beautifully rolled joint in his mouth, DENNIS *counts the money* WARREN *threw on the bed.*

WARREN

Two hundred.

DENNIS *finishes counting. From under the mattress he pulls a beat-up school composition notebook and flips through it till he finds Warren's name.*

DENNIS

"Warren."

He writes something in the book.

DENNIS (*Writing.*)
"*Cleared*, with stolen funds."

WARREN
They're not stolen, man, he gave it to me.

DENNIS *closes the book, finds a match, and lights up.*

DENNIS (*Holding in the smoke.*)
Where did Christian get this from?

WARREN
I don't know.

DENNIS *slaps* WARREN *in the face, playfully but hard.*

DENNIS
Don't fuckin' lie to me—where'd he get it?

WARREN *tries to hit* DENNIS *back. They scuffle, but* DENNIS *is much bigger and stronger and stops him.*

WARREN
Don't fuckin' hit me—

DENNIS
Where did he get it from?

WARREN
Why don't you ask him?

DENNIS
Did he get it from Philip?

WARREN
No, he said he got it from some fuckin' Rastafarian.

DENNIS
That guy Wally?

WARREN
I don't know.

> DENNIS

That guy Kresko?

> WARREN

I don't know. I don't keep track of where you guys perform your criminal activities. Who cares? Gimme that.

DENNIS *doesn't move. He keeps smoking.* WARREN *reaches for the joint.* DENNIS *allows him to take it.*

> DENNIS

How much money did you steal?

> WARREN

A lot.

> DENNIS

Let me see.

WARREN *opens his backpack and takes out a felt shoe bag stuffed with thousands of dollars in small bills. He loosens the ties and shows it to* DENNIS.

> DENNIS

That's a lot.

> WARREN

It's fifteen thousand dollars.

> DENNIS

Are you *fucking* crazy? (*Pause.*) Give me half.

> WARREN

No.

> DENNIS

Give me five.

> WARREN

I'm not giving you anything.

DENNIS

No. Give me five, we'll go to *France*, and we'll mail the rest back to your Dad with a note. "Took five. Went to *France*."

WARREN

I'm keeping it.

DENNIS

Are you kidding? He'll send large men after you with *guns*.

WARREN

He doesn't even know I have it.

DENNIS

What do you mean?

WARREN   DENNIS
I mean he—   Where did you *get* it from?

WARREN

It was in his room.

DENNIS

It was in his *room*?

WARREN

Yeah.

DENNIS

Your father keeps fifteen thousand dollars cash in his *room*? For what? *Tips*?

WARREN

I don't know. I guess he's got some kind of illicit lingerie deal in the works or something, I don't know.

DENNIS

Your father is so heavy, man . . .

WARREN

Yeah, so after he threw me out and went to *supper*, I was just roaming the house looking for liftable objects, if that was gonna be his attitude. So I go in his bedroom and there's this sinister looking *brief*case just *sitting* on his *bed*. So I jimmied open the lock and there's like rows and rows of cash just starin' at me. Like totally full of money.

DENNIS

Jason.

WARREN

Yeah! So I'm like, "*Dad* . . . !" And then I'm like, "Should I take this? This is some serious money." And then I'm like, "Fuck yeah. Make him *pay*." So I take out the cash, and I fill the briefcase with all these old National Geographics and lock it up again. So it'll probably sit there for the weekend, and then when he goes to deposit it, or bribe whoever he was planning on bribing, he'll open it up and hopefully he'll think like one of his *cohorts* ripped him off. Or like, his *slut* did it.

DENNIS

No he *won't*.

WARREN

Why not?

DENNIS

Of *course* he won't.

WARREN

Why not?

DENNIS

Because he's not a *moron*.

WARREN

Yes he is.

DENNIS

You really think after he throws you out of the house he's gonna open his briefcase and find twenty copies of his own National Geographics where his *money* should be, and he's not gonna know you did it? You're a fuckin' moron. Now get that shit outta here.

WARREN

I'm telling you—

DENNIS

Take it over to Christian's house and let your father's body-guards break *his* fuckin' legs.

WARREN

He doesn't *have* any bodyguards.

DENNIS

That guy who drives his car is not a bodyguard?

WARREN

No, he's a *driver.*

DENNIS

That guy like shows me his *gun*, like every time I *see* him.

WARREN

Yeah, because he's *insane.* But my father is not a *criminal.* He's just in *business* with criminals.

DENNIS

I don't give a shit *what* he is. I can't believe you cart that kind of money across town and like bring it to my *doorstep.* No—no—I mean you are so stupid, man, you are so incredibly stupid. He kicks you out so you steal fifteen thousand *dollars* from him?

WARREN

I was pissed.

DENNIS

OK: Get it out of here. Take it to Christian's house.

WARREN

He's not home.

DENNIS

Take it to Yoffie's house; go to Leonard's house. I don't care.

WARREN

Nobody's home. Everyone's parents are home. I'm not allowed in their houses. Come on. I don't want to be wandering around the streets with all that money. Come on.

Pause.

DENNIS

This is so typical of you, man, I mean this is like . . .

WARREN

Yeah yeah yeah.

DENNIS

This is like the prototype moronic move we've all come to expect from your corner. You drive the guy *crazy* because you're such a sniveling little obnoxious punk, you *grate* on the guy until he finally throws you out—arguably the most dangerous lingerie manufacturer in the *world*— And then you steal his money and bring it to my *house*, and expect me to like *hide* you or something?

WARREN (*Starts to speak.*)

DENNIS

No—no— That's why nobody likes you, man, because you're always provoking people. OK, now everybody's provoked, only *you're* the one they all fuckin' hate! Listen to me. I'm trying to tell you something. This is good for you.

WARREN

Oh, yeah.

DENNIS

No it is. It's good for you. Listen. You're a fuckin' *idiot*. You never have any money. Nobody can stand to have you around. And you can't get laid. I mean, man, you cannot get laid. You *never* get laid. Like the last girlfriend you had was in like ninth grade and it lasted for two weeks, and that bitch probably still hasn't recovered.

WARREN

She hasn't. I freaked her out.

DENNIS

What kind of *life* do you lead? You live with your father— a psycho. He beats the shit out of you on like this regular *basis*, you habitually owe me hundreds of dollars, you never pay me—until now, but we won't even discuss that— Nobody can stand to have you around because you're such an annoying loudmouthed little creep, and now you're like some kind of fugitive from *justice*? What is gonna happen to you, man?

WARREN

What's gonna happen to anybody? Who cares?

DENNIS *shrugs, sits. Relights the joint, which has gone out.*

WARREN

Like you're so independent?

DENNIS

Yeah, because my parents *pay* for this apartment. They don't throw me *out* of it. Because they're so grateful I don't wanna live with them. Because I don't *goad* them into *making* me dependent. I'm just like, "*Don't* send me to college. Just spring for my rent, I'll be a fuckin' *bike* messenger till I decide what I wanna do, and we'll never have to deal with each other." And they're like, "*Fine*."

Pause.

WARREN

Why do you say that shit?

DENNIS

Because it's true.

WARREN	DENNIS
Why do you—	Because you deserve it.

WARREN *is close to tears.*

DENNIS

Are you *crying* now?

WARREN

No. (*Pause.*) *I* don't know what to do. (*Pause.*) *I* don't know where to go.

DENNIS

Well—for one thing you should give me five thousand dollars and then you should return that money.

WARREN

I'm not giving you five thousand dollars.

DENNIS

I'm telling you. *France.*

Pause.

WARREN

You want some money?

DENNIS

No, I don't want any money.

WARREN *opens the bag and holds out two bricks of cash.*

WARREN

Take some money. Go to fuckin' France.

DENNIS

I don't wanna go to France. Like I want your father *stalking* me for the rest of my life? Now put that shit back in the bag and take it back to where you found it. It *scares* me.

WARREN *puts the money back and closes the ties.*

WARREN

I can't return it because he's home by now. He's *asleep.* The shit is in his bedroom and he's gonna be home all day tomorrow because he's having some associates over for *brunch.*

DENNIS

Brunch. (*Pause.*) That's a wild concept: It's not breakfast and it's not lunch. It's *brunch.* (*Rolls the word around in his mouth.*) "Brunch." "Let's serve *brunch . . .* " It's something you *serve.* (*Long pause.*) This is strong pot.

WARREN

I know.

DENNIS

All right: You know what you should tell your father?

WARREN

It doesn't matter what I do. He's gonna kill me anyway, so what's the difference?

DENNIS

No. Let's figure this out. It's gonna be OK. I'm a total mathematical genius. Now how much of this cash did you spend?

WARREN

Not much. I paid you back . . . I took a cab . . . I ate sushi . . . Two hundred and fifty bucks. But he gave me fifty.

DENNIS

OK. So don't spend any more, hang out till Monday, and

then return it on Monday when he goes to work. If the briefcase is already gone, then just like, leave the cash in his bedroom with a note of explanation—and like, leave town.

WARREN

I don't know.

DENNIS

That's a sound plan. And if he still hasn't even opened the briefcase you're like home free. Except for two hundred bucks.

WARREN

Can I get the two hundred back from you?

DENNIS

No, man, that's like, *paid.* I can't release that cash.

WARREN

Where am I gonna stay?

DENNIS

Stay with Christian.

WARREN

Why can't I stay here?

DENNIS

'Cause I don't want you.

WARREN

It's just two days.

DENNIS

I don't care.

WARREN

Come on. Nothing is gonna happen. He's not gonna know I came here. He definitely won't open the briefcase till Monday, and I'll be gone by then.

DENNIS

You are so stupid, man. I mean this definitely crowns your career as an idiot.

WARREN

Just let me stay here for Christ's sakes! I do shit for you all the time—

DENNIS

Like what?

WARREN

Like when your girlfriend kicked you out, you stayed at my house for two *weeks*—

DENNIS

That was your *father's* house.

WARREN

So *what*?

DENNIS

This is *my* house.

WARREN

And I got in a lotta trouble for that, too. I hang out with you whenever you want, I play sports with you all the time, I buy pot from you, I take all your fuckin' abuse and I'm a good fuckin' friend. So why can't you help me out when I'm in trouble and not be such a fuckin' asshole?

DENNIS

'Cause you're *always* in trouble. You have like no sense of *differentiation*.

WARREN

It's just two days!

DENNIS

All right, all right, shut up.

WARREN

Thanks.

DENNIS

But if your father shows up here I'm givin' you up immediately.

WARREN

I'm sure you will. But he's not gonna.

Silence.

WARREN

So what's up? What do you wanna do?

DENNIS

No, I don't wanna *do anything.* Don't *needle* me, Warren. If you wanna stay here you can stay here, but you gotta shut up.

DENNIS *turns on the TV and watches it wholeheartedly.*

WARREN

Hey, where's that chick Jessica? (*Pause.*) Denny. Have you seen that chick Jessica recently?

DENNIS

No. What about her?

WARREN

I'm into her.

DENNIS

She's out of your league, man.

WARREN

I think she likes me.

DENNIS

No she doesn't.

WARREN

I think she does.

DENNIS

Shut up.

WARREN

She's really cute, man.

DENNIS

She is cute. That's why it'll never happen.

WARREN *wanders over to the fridge.*

DENNIS

There's nothing in there.

WARREN *opens the fridge and looks in. It's pretty bare.*

DENNIS

Get *outta* there, Warren! I just told you there's nothing in there.

WARREN

How come you never have any food in here?

DENNIS *doesn't answer. He watches TV.*

WARREN

Let's go play football.

DENNIS *doesn't answer.*

WARREN

Where's your girlfriend?

DENNIS

We had a fight.

WARREN

Why?

DENNIS

Because she's a cunt

WARREN

Tell her to come over and bring that girl Jessica.

DENNIS

Tell her yourself.

WARREN (*Going to the phone*)

Where's she at?

DENNIS

You can't call her. We had a fight.

WARREN *picks up* DENNIS's *football and makes phantom passes.*

WARREN

Let's go outside and play.

DENNIS

Forget it.

WARREN

Let's call your girlfriend and tell her to call that girl Jessica, and we'll take a few thousand bucks out of the shoe bag and rent a really nice hotel suite and get a lot of champagne and shit and have a wild party. What do you think?

WARREN *throws* DENNIS *the football.* DENNIS *throws it back.* DENNIS *knows how to throw a football.*

DENNIS

You can't spend that money.

WARREN

I'll spend some of it. Big deal.

They toss the football back and forth.

WARREN

Come on, I'll get laid. It'll be good.

DENNIS

Let's just get a couple of prostitutes.

WARREN

OK.

DENNIS

You want to? We can call this Japanese place Philip goes to, and they'll send over like two incredibly beautiful and obedient Oriental hostesses to entertain and delight us.

WARREN

Let's do it.

DENNIS

How much will you spend?

WARREN

I don't know. How much is it?

DENNIS

Like two hundred apiece.

WARREN

I'd be into that.

DENNIS

What'll you tell your Dad?

WARREN

Fuck my Dad. I took his *money*!

DENNIS

You *robbed* him!

WARREN *throws a hard pass that goes wide and smashes into some breakables.*

WARREN

Whoa. Sorry.

DENNIS

What is your problem!?

WARREN

I lost control of the ball.

DENNIS *gets the ball out of the smashed shelfware.*

WARREN

Yo. Denny. Toss it back.

DENNIS

You broke my girlfriend's sculpture!

WARREN

Whoa . . . Really? I'm sorry.

DENNIS

What is your *problem*?

WARREN

I don't know. I really broke it?

DENNIS

Yeah, you really *broke* it.

WARREN *comes over and examines the broken clay sculpture.*

WARREN

What was it?

DENNIS

It was two girls, makin' out.

WARREN

Intense.

DENNIS

Now it's like, half of two girls.

WARREN

I'm really sorry, man, it was an accident.

DENNIS

It's a piece of shit anyway.

WARREN

Yo, lemme see it. Maybe I can glue it back together.

DENNIS

Get away from it.

WARREN

Lemme see.

WARREN *tries to get a hand on the broken sculpture.* DENNIS *roughly blocks him out with his body and elbows.*

DENNIS

Go sit in the *corner*, Warren, you're a fuckin' menace. Look what you *did.*

WARREN

Let me repair it.

DENNIS *can't do anything with it. He lets* WARREN *look at it.*

WARREN

No problem. You just get some Krazy Glue and glue it together. Do you have any?

DENNIS

No I don't have any *Krazy* Glue.

WARREN

I can fix this.

DENNIS *wanders away from the shelves.*

DENNIS

I'm *wasted* . . .

> WARREN

Look. See?

He has propped the two halves of the broken sculpture together so it looks whole.

> WARREN

Just glue it like that and it'll be fine. You probably don't even need a clamp.

WARREN *picks up the football and makes phantom passes at* DENNIS.

> WARREN

Yo, heads up. Yo, Denny—go out.

> DENNIS

Would you put that *down*?

> WARREN

Go long!

> DENNIS

The fuck am I gonna go *long*?

> WARREN

Yo, go out!

WARREN *throws the football hard, a little out of* DENNIS' *reach, and it smashes into a bunch of other stuff.*

> DENNIS

What is *with* you, Warren?

> WARREN

Come on, you *had* it!

DENNIS *grabs the football, rears back, and wings a viciously hard pass at* WARREN'*s head.* WARREN *ducks and the football smashes into the sculpture again, totally demolishing it.*

> DENNIS

Catch it, you *moron*! Don't *duck*! This is my *house*!

WARREN

You tried to kill me, man!

DENNIS

What is the matter with you?

WARREN

I didn't *do* anything!

DENNIS *stalks the room toward* WARREN, *grabs him in a headlock and flings him down on the floor. They are both half-laughing.*

DENNIS

Get outta my *house*!

WARREN

Come on, man, I didn't do anything!

DENNIS *rains open-handed blows down on* WARREN's *head and body.* WARREN *covers up.* DENNIS *drops onto his gut, knee first.* WARREN *groans in pain.* DENNIS *gets up and looks at the wreckage.*

DENNIS

Look what you did.

WARREN

Oh my stomach.

DENNIS

Oh, forget *this* . . .

He starts tossing the pieces of the sculpture, basketball-style, into the wastepaper basket across the room. He's a good shot. Most of them go in.

DENNIS

She's gonna freak out.

The last piece goes into the wastepaper basket. DENNIS *walks over to it and boots it into the wall. He goes to* WARREN, *who is covering his head.*

DENNIS

You all right?

WARREN *uncovers his head.* DENNIS *slaps him in the face.*

> WARREN
>
> Cut it out.

> DENNIS
>
> That's for breaking her shit.

> WARREN
>
> You murdered my stomach.

Long silence.

> WARREN
>
> I'm restless.

DENNIS *gives him a look.*

> WARREN
>
> So, you don't wanna call any Japanese hostesses?

> DENNIS
>
> You couldn't handle it. You'd go limp and be depressed about it for like a year and a half.

> WARREN
>
> Let's call 'em!

> DENNIS
>
> Shut up. It's two hundred dollars apiece. You wanna spend that cash?

> WARREN
>
> No, man, I can't.

> DENNIS
>
> What are you gonna do about the two hundred bucks?

> WARREN
>
> I don't know. I'll sell something.

DENNIS

What, from like your little faggot memorabilia collection?

WARREN

Yeah.

DENNIS

So why don't you ever sell any of that shit to pay *me*? You should let me call Adam Saulk's brother, man. He makes a fortune buying and selling that shit.

WARREN

I pay you.

DENNIS

You do not.

WARREN

Besides, paying you isn't like life and death. Anyway, you make so much money off all of us already it's like completely ridiculous.

DENNIS

Yeah, and I always smoke pot with you, all of you, *my* pot, all the time, like hundreds and hundreds of dollars' worth. So why shouldn't I make some money offa you? You fuckin' guys like *gripe* at me all the time, and I'm providing you schmucks with such a crucial service. Plus I'm developing valuable entrepreneurial skills for my future. *Plus* I'm like providing you with precious memories of your *youth*, for when you're fuckin' *old*. I'm like the basis of half your personality. All you do is imitate me. I turned you onto *The Honeymooners*, Frank *Zappa*, Ernst *Lubitsch*, *Sushi*. I'm like a one-man youth culture for you pathetic assholes. You're gonna remember your youth as like a gray stoned haze punctuated by a series of beatings from your fuckin' Dad, and like, *my* jokes. God *damn*! You know how much *pot* I've thrown out the *window* for you guys in the middle of the night when you're wandering around the street like *junkies* looking for half a joint so you can go to sleep, because you scraped all the *resin* out of

your pipes? And you bitch about the fact that along
the way I turn a little profit? You should thank
God you ever *met* me, you little fuckin' hero-worshipping
little *fag*.

WARREN

You are out of your mind, man.

DENNIS *laughs.* WARREN *opens his big suitcase and start removing the first items in an extensive collection of toys and memorabilia from the 1950s and '60s: Mint condition mid-'60s Matell toys, first release albums, a 1950s toaster, etc.*

DENNIS

Don't take that stuff out in here.

WARREN

Why not? I wanna see what I can sell.

DENNIS

No—no— Don't take that stuff out in my apartment. It depresses me.

WARREN

Why?

DENNIS

Don't take all that cutesy kitschy fuckin' retro-Sixties bull-shit out in my apartment. I don't wanna look at it.

WARREN

I can get a couple of hundred bucks for any of these albums.

DENNIS

Lemme see.

WARREN *hands him an obscure early Frank Zappa album.*

DENNIS

Where'd you get this?

WARREN
From this buddy of mine in Seattle.

DENNIS
This is an amazing album.

DENNIS *looks through some of the stuff.*

DENNIS
What is this shit? What's with the little *spacemen*? You are weird, man.

WARREN
This is Major Matt Mason. Don't you remember this?

DENNIS
No.

WARREN
They had these when we were little. They're really cool, and these are in really good condition. I could get like a hundred fifty, two hundred bucks for this.

DENNIS
Seriously?

WARREN
Yeah.

DENNIS
So how do you always owe me money?

WARREN
'Cause I don't wanna sell them.

DENNIS
You are a depressing little man. Now put that shit away.

WARREN (*Holding it out to him.*)
Look, he's got a little space helmet. The visor moves up and down.

DENNIS

Get that shit *away* from me!

The phone rings. DENNIS *lets it ring twice, then picks up.*

DENNIS (*Into the phone.*)

Yeah? . . . Because you're bein' a cunt.

The line goes dead. DENNIS *hangs up and laughs, suddenly energized.*

WARREN

You're intense, man.

DENNIS

I'm the best! I don't let people freak me out. I freak *them* out.

WARREN

You're an amazing man.

DENNIS

Hey—listen: That girl you like: what's her name?

WARREN

Jessica.

DENNIS

She's friends with that other girl, Natalie. You know her?

WARREN

Yeah?

DENNIS

OK, check it out: That girl Natalie likes me, OK? Last summer when Valerie was in Sweden with her family, I was like making out with her all the time, but that's all she ever let me do. But I saw her last week and she was coming onto me all over the place. So look: new plan: We'll take a thousand bucks out of the shoe bag, cab it over to Philip's house, pick up an ounce of blow, call Natalie, tell her and Jessica to come over here, we'll get them wired, I'll fuck Natalie—you do your best to fuck Jessica— Then tomorrow we make a few calls, sell the rest of the blow, turn a tidy little profit, and return the whole fifteen grand to your psychotic father intact on Monday. That's a great plan.

WARREN

How do you figure?

DENNIS

Because we extract a quarter ounce for ourselves, throw back in a quarter ounce of cut, sell it for like a hundred twenty-five a gram, clear around thirty-six hundred bucks, return the thousand dollar investment to the bag along with the two hundred you already owe him, and you're still gonna end up making like six hundred dollars.

WARREN (*Slowly.*)

. . . All right . . .

DENNIS

OK?

WARREN

Yeah.

DENNIS (*Grabbing the phone.*)

OK—

WARREN

But like . . . what's the basic margin of profit?

DENNIS

Like eighteen hundred each.

WARREN

So but . . . if we're making eighteen hundred each, how come I only end up with *six*?

DENNIS (*Still holding the phone.*)

You *don't* end up with six: you end up with *eighteen*, minus the thousand you're investing and the two hundred you already *owe*. Plus a free eighth of blow, which you can snort or sell as you see fit. Get it?

                    WARREN
Um, not really. But whatever.

                    DENNIS
What don't you get?

                    WARREN
I don't really get the whole thing.

DENNIS *hangs up the phone.*

                    DENNIS
Look: We're buying a Z for a *thousand dollars* . . .

                    WARREN
No, I get *that* part. I just—I mean, theoretically, we're making a joint investment, right?

                    DENNIS
Yeah . . . ?

                    WARREN
Only in terms of the actual cash outlay, it's all coming from my area. Right? So in a way, I'm the only actual investor.

                    DENNIS
Yeah . . . ?

                    WARREN
So then why aren't I making all the money?

                    DENNIS
Because it's my connect and my customers and I'm gonna have the shit in my house.

                    WARREN
Yeah, but—

DENNIS

What do you *mean* why aren't you making all the money?

WARREN

I'm not saying I *should*. But you're saying we should split the profits *before* I put back the thousand dollars, and I'm saying like, why aren't we doing it *afterwards*?

DENNIS

Because it's my *connect*. I'm providing the *connect*.

WARREN

I'm providing the *cash*.

DENNIS

So what?

WARREN

. . . So I figure the odds be fifty-fifty.

DENNIS

You do, huh? All right. Whatever . . . But that's fucked up, because I'm doing all the work, and all you did was steal some money from your father which you're getting back in like ten *minutes*.

WARREN

All right, so what do you want to do?

DENNIS

I don't know. I just—I should definitely get some kind of *service* fee. So look—we'll split the twenty-six hundred net: thirteen hundred each. And then you pay me two hundred more for doing all the *work*—that leaves me with fifteen and you with eleven hundred. Out of which you can pay your father back the two hundred dollars or not. Whatever you want. OK?

WARREN

I guess.

DENNIS

Is that all *right* with you? Can I *call* him now?

WARREN

Yeah. Call him up.

DENNIS

Don't *ever* try to out-Jew me, little man. I'm twice the Jew
you'll *ever* be. I'm like a Jewish *god*. I'm like—*Joooo*olius
Caesar!

WARREN

You're a fuckin' *mental* case, man.

DENNIS

Way to take care of *business*, little Warren!

DENNIS *pinches* WARREN *very hard.*

WARREN

Ow!

DENNIS *dials the phone. Waits.*

DENNIS (*To* WARREN.)

He's not there. (*Into the phone.*) Philly. Dennis. Call me.
I'm looking for some fun.

He hangs up.

DENNIS

Shit.

The phone rings. He lets it ring twice, then picks up.

DENNIS (*Into the phone.*)

Yeah? . . . No! . . . 'Cause I don't know! . . . 'Cause I don't
give a shit . . . Yeah . . . Yeah, OK . . . (*To* WARREN.) Go in
the bathroom.

WARREN

Come on . . .

DENNIS
Go in the bathroom!

WARREN *goes in the bathroom.*

DENNIS (*Into the phone.*)
I'm sorry, baby. I know I messed up . . . I know! As soon
as I start arguing, I immediately snap into attack mode
and just become as insanely brutal as I possibly can. It's
because of my fuckin' *mother* . . . All right, why don't you
come over? . . . Warren's here, but I'll get rid of him . . .
Yeah . . . Oh, *really*? . . . No, totally *bring* her: Warren's
like, in *love* with her . . . Would she be into that? . . . What
if we got some blow? . . . She might. All right. See if she'll
come over. I'll work on it.

DENNIS *hangs up.*

DENNIS
Hey!

WARREN *comes out of the bathroom.*

WARREN
What's up?

DENNIS
Nothin'. I got good news for you, so get your little boner
ready, 'cause my girlfriend's on her way over with your
favorite teenage prostitute.

WARREN
What do you mean?

DENNIS
What do you think I mean?

WARREN
She's with Jessica?

DENNIS
Yeah.

                    WARREN
They're coming over here?

                    DENNIS
That's right, my little love machine.

                    WARREN
Excellent.

                    DENNIS
Only I told 'em we'd get drugs, so shut up for a second and
let me think.

Pause. He picks up the phone and dials.

                    WARREN
Who are you calling?

DENNIS *ignores him.*

                DENNIS (*Into the phone.*)
Stuey. Hey. What are you doing? . . . You are too much,
man. You shoulda been like, a Roman *Senator.* Let me ask
you something: Have you seen this weed Christian's been
selling? It's like an olive-colored dark green heavy sense
with like a medium amount of fuzz, very wet and sticky,
in like long oblong-shaped little buds, shaped like beef
sate . . . Oh you got some? . . . Do you know where he got
it? . . . All right: Let me ask you something else. Do you
know where Philip is? . . . Yeah. Have you seen it? . . . How
is it? . . . *Really.* How much did you get? . . . What's he asking? . . . I did. He's not home . . . No, I just *tried* him, you
fat fuck, he's *not home.* Why do you have to aggravate me
all the time?

                    WARREN
What's up?

                DENNIS (*Into the phone.*)
So listen. Stuey. Baby: If I can't get ahold of Philip in like
twenty, I'm comin' over there and taking an eighth offa

you, all right? . . . No, *Stuart*, I'm not *buying* it from you,
I'm *taking* it, at cost. I'll give you cash up front, whatever
you paid Philip, and you can get more from him tomorrow
. . . *Yeah*, as a *favor* . . . Because I'm *asking* you to, that's
why. Because I fuckin' *introduced* you to him in the first
place, you fuckin' globulous *fuck*. You wouldn't even *know*
him if it wasn't for me: you'd still be dealing commercial
pot outside some Long Island mall to a bunch of dyed-
blonde Great Neck *bimbettes*, you fat fuckin' asshole. I
created you, Stuey, and I can destroy you just as easily! I
don't care how many syphilis-ridden Dutch backpackers
are blowing you, man. Why do you always have to like, try
to have some mincing little bullshit *advantage* over me all
the time? So you don't feel like such a fat, ugly *man* or
something? . . . No, man, because you're like totally unciv-
ilized. You have like no sense of protocol, like whatsoever
. . . All right all right. I'll call you back.

He hangs up.

WARREN

What's up?

DENNIS

Nothin'. He's sitting on his waterbed doing *speed*balls with
some naked Dutch *hitch*hiker he picked up at the *bus*
stop, and he wants to like *dicker* with me over the price of
an eighth of coke, like I can't go over to Philip's myself
tomorrow and pick it up for *less* than what *he* paid, and
like I haven't turned him on to tons of business and tons
of my own customers—just so he can be holding some
kind of *cards* on me or something. Plus he's so stoned out
of his mind to begin with you can't understand a word he's
saying anyway.

WARREN

So . . . what are we gonna do?

DENNIS

I don't know. See if Philip calls back, and if he doesn't,
we'll just have to deal with the Fat Man. Maybe we should

just forget it. It's late anyway. I don't wanna be lying in bed grinding my teeth all night. Unless you wanna just stay up and watch "H.R. Pufnstuff" at 5:30 in the morning.

WARREN

I can't watch that show, man. It freaks me out.

DENNIS

So what do you wanna do?

WARREN

Well . . . Are they coming over?

DENNIS

Yeah they're coming over.

WARREN

I'm into it.

DENNIS

All right. Should we get heroin? No, too much, right?

WARREN

Let's do speedballs.

DENNIS

Shut up. Do you even *know* what a speedball *is*? No.

WARREN

Yeah I know what a speedball is. It's like half heroin half cocaine. Right?

DENNIS

Yeah, but we can't give these girls *speed*balls. What are you, a maniac? Anyway, Valerie won't do heroin. *You* won't do heroin. So what are you talking about?

WARREN

I've done it.

DENNIS

Yeah, *once*. You'd be throwing up all night. That'd make a good impression. Speedballs are *sick*, man. They get you so fucked up you're like, really sorry.

WARREN

Let's do it!

DENNIS

Shut up.

Long pause.

WARREN

What's up?

DENNIS

No, nothing's *up*. How can you sit in a room with some-body for hours with nothing going on, and keep asking "What's up?" every ten minutes like something *new* hap-pened all of a sudden that you didn't know about?

WARREN

I don't know. It's just an expression.

WARREN *is walking around the room, picking things up and looking at them.*

WARREN

So what's up? Where are they?

DENNIS

They're coming. Take it easy. And get away from my shit.

WARREN *keeps looking through* DENNIS's *stuff.*

WARREN

But do they know I'm here?

DENNIS

Yeah, yeah, I told 'em you're here, I totally set it up for you. Just don't get weird and bizarre and start talking about your dead sister, and you'll do fine.

WARREN
I'm not gonna talk about anything.

Pause.

DENNIS
Yeah, just don't be like—

WARREN
You're really harsh, man.

DENNIS
I'm harsh?

WARREN
Yeah.

DENNIS
Why? You should *face* that shit.

WARREN
I face it all the time.

DENNIS
Well why do you have like her childhood *pictures* up all over your room, and like articles about her *murder* in your fuckin' *drawer*, like ten years after the fact? You're gonna let that shit dominate your life? You gotta like, get *on* with it.

WARREN
I am getting on with it. That's why I have her picture up. So I can get on with it. (*Pause.*) She's fuckin' lucky she's dead anyway.

DENNIS
She is not. Shut up.

Pause. DENNIS *gets up and goes to his stereo and puts on a record. It is a slow song, e.g., Frank Zappa's "Any Way the Wind Blows," from* Ruben and The Jets. *He holds out his arms and walks toward* WARREN, *singing along to him loudly.*

WARREN

Get away from me.

DENNIS *keeps coming, looming over* WARREN, *who tries to escape.*

WARREN

Get away from me, man.

DENNIS *falls on top of him, crushing him with his body, still singing.*

WARREN

Get *off* me, man!

DENNIS *laughs, screams.* WARREN *struggles to get out from under him.* DENNIS *gives him a loud wet kiss on the cheek and sits back.* WARREN *pushes him over and sits up.* DENNIS *flops onto his back.* WARREN *walks around.*

DENNIS

I love Warren, man. He plays with me all day and all night for as long as I want and he never complains.

He sits up, grabs the phone, and dials.

DENNIS (*Into the phone.*)

Stuey. It's me. I'm comin' over: What are you telling me? . . . OK, *forget* it.

WARREN

What's up?

DENNIS (*Covering the phone.*)

He'll only sell us an ounce for fifteen hundred if you give him the cash up front. So I'm not doing that. I don't buy retail. But you can, if you want. But I'm not paying this *pork* loin fifteen hundred bucks for an ounce of blow. It's not worth my while.

WARREN

So let's—

DENNIS

Unless, we just keep an *eighth* for ourselves, instead of a quarter. That way you still make your eleven hundred and I make my fifteen. We just keep less blow for ourselves. (*Into the phone.*) HOLD ON A SECOND! (*Covers the phone.*) So what do you want to do?

WARREN

I'd go for it.

DENNIS (*Into the phone.*)

All right, I'm comin' over. Get dressed.

He hangs up and starts looking for his sneakers.

WARREN

So should we get some champagne or something?

DENNIS

All right. But I'm not payin' for that either.

WARREN

Nobody's asking you to.

DENNIS

What do you want, like Dom Perignon?

WARREN

There is no other brand.

DENNIS

How many should I get? One bottle? Two?

WARREN

Let's get two.

DENNIS

They're expensive.

WARREN

That's no problem.

DENNIS

All right.

WARREN

So . . . how much do you need?

DENNIS

Gimme fifteen hundred for the blow and like two hundred for the champagne.

WARREN

The champagne's not gonna cost two hundred dollars.

DENNIS

Just gimme enough to cover it. Or let's just forget the whole thing. I don't wanna do any coke. It's a terrible drug. It's for chumps. It sucks. I'll fuck my girlfriend and go to sleep, and you can go sleep in the park.

Pause. WARREN *goes to the shoe bag and starts counting out the money.* DENNIS *starts putting on his sneakers.*

WARREN

So but . . . should I come with you, or what's the deal?

DENNIS

No, you gotta let Valerie in. She threw her key down the trash chute.

WARREN

No, man . . . I don't wanna deal with your girlfriend.

DENNIS

It's all right. We made up. Just stay here. I won't be long.

WARREN

Whatever.

DENNIS *finishes tying his sneakers and looks at him.*

DENNIS

See—this is no good. You're already like freaked out and nervous. Forget it. That girl's gonna smell it the minute she comes in. What is the *matter* with you?

WARREN

What do you mean?

DENNIS

What are you, like, worried about what to *say*? Don't say *any*thing. Just sit there and look handsome, you Greek *god*. She should be worried about *you*. You're a handsome guy. You're like an intelligent fuckin' interesting guy. You don't have to *do* anything. Just don't get freaked out. We're gonna break this stupefying losing streak of yours wide open. Now gimme the money.

WARREN

All right. (*Pointedly.*) This is *seventeen hundred.*

DENNIS (*Mocking his grave tone.*)
"All right."

DENNIS *takes the money and shuffles into his coat.*

DENNIS

So just let 'em up and I'll be back in like twenty.

WARREN

Cool.

DENNIS

Be *glad*, man! She's really cute and she's got a great body and maybe you can actually fuck her.

WARREN

I'm gonna give it the old college try.

DENNIS *goes out.* WARREN *locks the door after him. Steps back into the room, alone. He looks at himself in the mirror. He tries to make his appearance more casual, but it's a challenge. He untucks his shirt, musses his hair, etc. He finds the half-smoked joint, lights it, and takes one huge hit.*

He sits there without moving.

The buzzer buzzes. He waits for it to buzz again before getting up to press the intercom button.

WARREN

Hello?

JESSICA (On the intercom.)

It's Jessica.

WARREN

OK.

WARREN *buzzes her in and moves away from the intercom. He waits. There is a knock on the door. He goes to the door, opens it, and steps back.*

WARREN

You may enter.

Enter JESSICA GOLDMAN *She is the same age as* WARREN—*around nineteen. She wears effective makeup, big shoes, and a slightly pricey little dress that shows off her figure to good advantage. She is dressed up for the night, not down, and definitely looks a little out of place in* DENNIS'*s grunge palace. She is a fairly cheerful but very nervous girl, whose self-taught method of coping with her nervousness consists of seeking out the nearest available oasis of self-assurance and entrenching herself there with a watchful defensiveness that sweeps away anything that might threaten to dislodge her, including her own chances at happiness and the opportunity of gaining a wider perspective on the world that might eventually make her less nervous to begin with. Despite her prickliness, she is basically friendly, definitely interested in* WARREN, *and trying to make a good impression.*

JESSICA

Hi, Warren. How are you?

WARREN

I'm OK.

He hesitates, then leans in to kiss her hello, on the cheek. She is not expecting this, so it's a little physically embarrassing.

WARREN

Um . . . Where's Valerie?

JESSICA

She went with *Dennis.* We ran into him downstairs, and they said I should just come *up.*

She stands by the door, not sure where to go or what's appropriate.

WARREN

So how you doing, Jessica? You're looking very automated tonight.

JESSICA

What the fuck is *that* supposed to mean?

WARREN

Nothing. It's just a fashion concept.

JESSICA

What?

WARREN

Um—nothing. You wanna come in?

She steps into the room. He closes the door.

JESSICA

So how long do you think they're gonna be?

WARREN

I don't know. Maybe a half-hour?

JESSICA

What? What do you mean? Where do they have to go?

WARREN

Like, the East Fifties.

JESSICA

Well . . . OK. (*Pause.*) I don't mean to be paranoid. I just don't want to be the victim of some teenage matchmaking scheme.

WARREN

Noted.

JESSICA

You know? If I'm gonna get set up, I'm gonna do it myself.

WARREN

Well nobody's setting you up, so why don't you calm down?

JESSICA

Oh you can't see why I would *think* that?

WARREN

I don't know or care what you think, Jessica. I'm just staying here because my *Dad* threw me out of the *house.* But go *home.* It's fine with me.

JESSICA (*Not an apology.*)

OK, *sorry.*

She comes in.

JESSICA

You probably think I'm like a total bitch now, right?

WARREN

I don't think anything. I don't even know what you're *talking* about.

He locks the door.

WARREN

And now . . . you're *mine*!

JESSICA

No *way*!

WARREN

I'm kidding! Calm *down*!

JESSICA (*On "calm."*)

That's not funny at *all*!

WARREN

Noted.

JESSICA *sits down and takes out her cigarettes and lighter.*

JESSICA

Is it OK if I smoke in here?

WARREN

Go ahead. It's not my house.

JESSICA

Well is there an ashtray or something I can use?

WARREN

I'm sure there's one somewhere.

He looks for an ashtray and finds one at the same time she finds an empty soda can.

WARREN

Here you go.

JESSICA

No, it's OK. I can use this. Thanks, though.

WARREN *puts down the ashtray and sits down across the room from her. She smokes.*

Long silence.

WARREN

So are you like a really big cigarette smoker?

JESSICA

I guess so.

WARREN

How many cigarettes would you say you smoke in the average day?

JESSICA

I don't know. Like a pack and a half a day, on a really heavy smoking day. Maybe like a half a pack a day if I'm like, in the country.

WARREN

. . . Yeah . . . I never really got into the whole cigarette scene myself. But I hear great things about it.

JESSICA

Well, but if you smoke pot all the time, it's much worse on your lungs than cigarettes.

WARREN

I guess my lungs are pretty severely damaged.

JESSICA

I'm sure they are.

Long silence.

JESSICA

So did those guys go to get, um, to get coke?

WARREN

That's the plan.

JESSICA

I don't want to do very much.

WARREN

Well, we're getting like, a *lot*.

JESSICA

I'll do *some* . . .

WARREN

And we're getting some Dom Perignon to top it off. So it should be pretty good.

JESSICA

Sounds good . . .

Long silence.

JESSICA

So why'd your Dad throw you out of the house? What did you *do*?

WARREN

We just had a slight policy dispute. It's no big deal.

JESSICA

Are you staying here? Where are you gonna sleep?

WARREN

I don't know. It wasn't like a really detailed plan. I was just planning to crash on the floor for a few days till I figure out what I'm doing.

JESSICA

What *are* you gonna do?

WARREN

I don't know. I was thinking I might just buy a bus ticket and head out West. I have a buddy who lives in Seattle, so I might just do that . . . I definitely wanna get out of *this—pit*. That's for sure.

JESSICA

You mean New York? You don't like living here?

WARREN

What's to like? You go outside and it *smells* bad. You know? And I live on Central Park *West*.

JESSICA

Well—

WARREN

I like the *out*doors.

JESSICA

I know, but—

WARREN

Like last winter I went to visit this buddy of mine who lives in Jackson Hole? In Wyoming? And we'd just *ski* every day, you know? And bus tables at night. And when you get up in the morning and open the front door it's like, *silent*. You know? You go outside and it's like, the *mountains*. And *snow*. And nobody around for *miles*. And like the whole . . . *sky* over your head. You know? So what the fuck am I doing languishing on *this* trash heap for? The intellectual stimulation? I'm not getting any. All I do is smoke pot. I can do that anywhere. I can just bring that *with* me, you know?

JESSICA

Yeah . . . I don't really take advantage of the city's facilities either, and it just seems like such a total waste.

WARREN

Yeah. I mean . . . yeah.

Pause.

JESSICA

But—you're not planning on going to school at all? Didn't you *go* to school somewhere or something?

WARREN

Um, briefly.

JESSICA

So . . . ?

WARREN

I . . . It just wasn't happening.

JESSICA

Where were you?

WARREN

Ohio.

JESSICA

Where, Oberlin?

WARREN

Whatever. You're at F.I.T., right?

JESSICA

Yeah. I really like it there. It's a little Jappy for me, but there's a lot of really great people there if you know where to look for them. But it's kind of weird, because I'm living at home— Which is great: like my Mom and I get along incredibly well—but a lot of my formerly closest "friends" are out of the city now, and sometimes I wonder, you know, if I should've . . . I don't know.

WARREN

So are you heavily into fashion development?

JESSICA

Yeah. I've been doing a lot of designing. I've always done it. It's what I want to do.

WARREN

Well . . . My basic philosophy about clothes is that they should be comfortable, and not look like too many people had to slave over their creation. But then again, I'm not very fashion-oriented.

JESSICA

Yeah, but, you know, you will be someday.

WARREN

I doubt it.

JESSICA

Yeah, but you will. Your whole personality'll be different.

WARREN

You think?

JESSICA

Sure. What you're like now has nothing to do with what you're gonna *be* like. Like right now you're all like this rich little pot-smoking burnout rebel, but ten years from now you're gonna be like a plastic *surgeon* reminiscing about how wild you used to be . . .

WARREN

Well, I don't want to make any rash predictions at this point . . . but I seriously doubt I'm gonna be going in for plastic surgery.

JESSICA

Well, OK, whatever, but you'll definitely be a completely different person. Everything you think will be different, and the way you act, and all your most passionately held beliefs are all gonna be completely different, and it's really depressing.

WARREN

How do you figure?

JESSICA

Because it just basically invalidates whoever you are right *now*. You know what I mean? It just makes your whole self at any given point in your life seem so completely *dismissable*. So it's like, what is the point?

WARREN

I don't really know about that . . .

JESSICA

Well it's *true*.

WARREN

Maybe so, but I don't really *agree* with it.

JESSICA

Well, I've thought about this a lot.

WARREN

So have I.

JESSICA

I mean look who our *President* is now if you don't believe
me.

WARREN

I'm not sure I follow you.

JESSICA

No, like the classic *example* is all those kids from the
Sixties who were so righteous about changing the face of
civilization, and then the minute they got older they were
all like, "Actually, you know what? Maybe I'll just be a
lawyer."

WARREN

I guess that's one interpretation . . .

JESSICA

But it's totally true! And now like Ronald *Reagan* is
President of the United States. I mean, how embarrassing
is *that*?

WARREN

It's pretty embarrassing . . . Although I have to say, I definitely know some people who are still seriously into civic
activities. Like my mother does a fair amount of volunteer
work for some kind of grape-picking civil-liberties organization in California . . .

JESSICA

I know people who do that too. But I'm not talking about
the last pathetic remnants of—Upper West Side Jewish . . .
liberalism. I'm talking about the *main*stream, and it
is such a *joke*. I mean, I definitely feel that *evil* has like,
triumphed in our time.

WARREN

So do I. But I still don't know if I would really ascribe all that to the theory that people's personalities undergo some kind of fundamental *alteration* when they get older.

JESSICA

Well, they do. And it's a big factor.

WARREN

I mean they obviously do to a *degree*—

JESSICA

Yeah!

WARREN

And things definitely happen to alter your general *trajectory*—

JESSICA

Yeah! And no matter—

WARREN (*On "And."*)

But I think that . . . you basically get a set of characteristics, and then they pretty much just develop in different ways. Like—

JESSICA

But can I just—

WARREN (*On "can."*)

Like the last year of high school, I suddenly realized that all these weird kids I grew up with were like well on their way to becoming really weird *adults*. And it was pretty *scary*, you know? Like you see a crazy kid, and you realize, he's never gonna grow *out* of it. He's a fucked-up crazy kid and he's just gonna be a fucked-up crazy adult with like a ruined life.

(*Pause.*)

JESSICA

Are you done now?

WARREN

I'm done with *that* thought.

JESSICA

Well can I please say something?

WARREN

Go ahead.

JESSICA

Thank you: I'm not saying anything about whether you're quote unquote "fucked up" or not. I don't mean it as a *moral* issue—

WARREN

Neither do I.

JESSICA

I just—

WARREN

I think that personality components are like protons and electrons. Like in science: Every molecule is made of the same basic components, like the difference between a hydrogen molecule and a calcium molecule is like *one proton* or something . . .

JESSICA

Yeah? That's wrong, but yeah?

WARREN

So my theory is that people's *personalities* are basically constructed the same way. None of them are exactly the same, but they're all made of the same thing.

JESSICA

That's interesting.

WARREN

Thank you.

JESSICA

Unfortunately it has nothing to do with what I'm *talking* about . . .

WARREN

That is unfortunate.

JESSICA

I'm not talking about the chemical structure of your *brain*, I'm talking about— It's like, when you find an old *letter* you wrote, that you don't remember writing. And it's got all these thoughts and opinions in it that you don't remember having, and it's written to somebody you don't even remember having ever written a letter *to*.

WARREN

I've never found a letter like that.

JESSICA

Well I have. Like, a lot of them. And it just makes you realize that there's just these huge swaths of time in your life that didn't register at *all*, and that you might just as well have been *dead* during them for all the difference they make to you now.

WARREN

That seems like a fairly nihilistic viewpoint, Jessica.

JESSICA

Well, I am so completely the opposite of nihilistic it's amazing that anyone could even *say* that about me.

WARREN

Well—

JESSICA

But we don't agree. So that's OK. You think what you think, and I think what I think, and there's no way we're ever going to convince each other, so my suggestion is we just drop it.

WARREN

All right.

Silence.

JESSICA

Hey, is there anything to drink in here? I've got this really bad taste in my mouth.

WARREN *(Getting up.)*

I think there's some water.

JESSICA *(Starts to get up.)*

I can get it.

WARREN

That's all right. "Chivalry is not dead. It just smells funny."

JESSICA *does not know how to respond to this, so she just looks at him. He gives up and goes to the fridge, finds a juice jar full of cold water, pours some in a glass, and brings it to her.*

JESSICA

Thanks a lot.

She takes the glass and drinks.

JESSICA

God, I was so thirsty.

WARREN *sits down, this time right next to her on the bed. He is sitting next to her, but not looking at her. It's making them both very nervous.* JESSICA *gets up and goes to the wall of photographs.*

JESSICA

So who are all these photos of? Are you on this wall?

WARREN

Yeah, I'm represented.

He follows her to the wall. She finds a photo with him in it.

JESSICA

Wow, is this *you*?

WARREN

Yep.

JESSICA

God, what a little *stoner.* You look so different with long hair . . .

WARREN

Yeah. Everybody definitely went for the traditional post-high-school chop.

JESSICA

Valerie says you just cut your hair when Dennis cut his hair.

WARREN *does not respond.*

JESSICA

Well, you definitely look better with it short.

WARREN

That seems to be the general consensus. But it makes me wanna like *instantly* have long hair.

JESSICA *scans the photographs.*

JESSICA

Wow. What a great picture of Dennis. I mean, he definitely has a slight cleanliness problem, but if he didn't, he'd be seriously gorgeous.

WARREN

You think?

JESSICA

Oh my God, are you *kidding*?

WARREN

I guess.

JESSICA

So his Dad's like a really famous painter, right?

WARREN

I guess he's pretty famous.

JESSICA

Wow. So is that like, really hard for Dennis to deal with?

WARREN

I have no idea.

JESSICA

And his father's really sick or something?

WARREN

Uh . . . He's definitely having some pretty dire prostate problems.

JESSICA

His Mom is beautiful . . .

WARREN

It's an incredibly attractive family.

JESSICA

What does she do?

WARREN

She's like a big city social-worker administrator of some kind. She's always like installing swimming pools for the poor or something.

JESSICA

What?

WARREN

Nothing. She runs these programs for the city government or something. She designs social-work programs for street kids and drug addicts and stuff like that. But she's a fuckin' psycho.

JESSICA (*Bristling.*)

Why do you say that? Just because she's a social worker?

WARREN

No—because of her *behavior.*

JESSICA
Why? What does she do?

WARREN
I don't know. She's just really *strident*. She's like a bleeding-heart dominatrix with like a *hairdo*. She—

JESSICA
"Bleeding heart?"

WARREN
I don't know. Yeah!

JESSICA
What are you like a big *Republican* or something?

WARREN
Not at all. I'm a total Democrat. I just—

JESSICA
So why do you *say* that about her?

WARREN
Because that's what's she's *like*. But I don't really *care*. Maybe she's really nice. I don't really want to get into an argument about it.

JESSICA
No, it's just—my sister is a social worker, and I really—

WARREN
I didn't say anything *about* your sister.

JESSICA
I know you didn't.
I just th—

WARREN
I didn't know you *had*
a sister.

I know—but I just think it's
like a really good thing to
do with your life and I j—
OK, I *know*! I just admire
people who dedicate
themselves like that, and I—

And I was not attempting to
vilify the entire social-worker
community!

WARREN

So do *I*. What she *does* is fine. It's just how she *is*. I think it's totally brave to do that kind of work. Unless you're just—

JESSICA

Unless what?

WARREN

Unless you just have no sense of people. No— Like if your *mission* overrides your actual moral *opinion*, but—forget it. It's not—it doesn't matter.

JESSICA

All right. I certainly didn't mean to offend you.

WARREN

I'm not offended.

A moment. JESSICA *looks at the stuff in* WARREN's *open suitcase.*

JESSICA

Hey—what's this stuff?

WARREN

Those are just some of my belongings.

JESSICA (*Looking through.*)

What are these?

WARREN

It's just some fuckin' shit.

JESSICA

What are these, like antique toys or something?

WARREN

Um, for the most part . . .

JESSICA

These are really cool.

WARREN

You think?

JESSICA

Yeah, they remind me of the stuff my cousins had when I was a little kid. I always wanted to play with their toys, and they were like, "Go play with dolls, you little bitch." And I was like, "Fuck *you!*" . . . I *love* old toys.

WARREN

I have a fair amount of this kind of thing.

JESSICA

Do you know how many toys I had—I mean how much, of the stuff I had when I was little, I wish I had now? Like, I think of some of those toys and I just look back on them with this *longing* . . . You know?

WARREN

Definitely.

JESSICA (*Takes out the Major Matt Masons.*)
Who are these guys?

WARREN

That's my Major Matt Mason collection. You know Major Matt Mason?

She shakes her head.

WARREN

Come on, Major Matt Mason, when we were kids—Aw, he's the best! Check him out, he's like, ready for his *mission.* I have a complete set, all in prime condition. I could actually sell them for a lot of money, but I'm hanging onto them.

JESSICA

Really cool.

He shows her his heavy-duty 1950s toaster.

WARREN
And this is my amazing toaster. Toaster Amazing, I call it.
Look at this. It's really something. (*She looks.*) Yeah, G.E.
made only like a few hundred of this model like in the
Fifties, and then they recalled them because they were
like exploding in people's kitchens at breakfast and burn-
ing down their homes. (*He laughs, sobers.*) So only a few
hundred actually exist. I got one from this dealer I know
in Colorado and he had *no* idea what he was selling me.

JESSICA
Huh.

WARREN
I have made toast with it, but nothing bad happened to
me. But I don't really use it too much because it really
depreciates in value. But it's great to know I have one of
the only ones in existence.

JESSICA
What's your favorite thing in this collection?

WARREN
Definitely my Wrigley Field Opening Day baseball cap
my grandfather gave me. No contest.

JESSICA
What's that?

WARREN *takes out an ancient blue and white baseball cap.*

WARREN
This is a real collectors' item, like an *amazing* collectors' item,
actually. My Mom's Dad got it the first day at Wrigley Field
when he was totally like a little kid, in nineteen-fourteen.

JESSICA *reads what's embroidered on the cap.*

JESSICA
"Wrigley Field, Home of the Chicago Cubs, Opening
Day." (*Reads off the other side.*) "True Value."

WARREN

True Value Hardware, all *right*.

She puts the hat on.

WARREN

Looks good, Jessica . . .

She smiles. A moment.

JESSICA

I didn't know your family was from Chicago.

WARREN

They're not. Just my grandfather. He was actually really
cool. When he was a young man, he was like a fairly well-
known aviator. You know, with like the fur-lined leather
cap with the earflaps, and the whole bit. He actually
set a couple of early endurance records in the nineteen-
twenties . . .

JESSICA

Wow . . . I didn't know that . . .

WARREN

Yeah . . . he was pretty interesting. (*He laughs.*) Like
whenever he would meet one of my friends, I'd be like,
"Grampa, this is my friend Neil." And my Grampa'd
be like, "Nice to meet you, Neil. Are you Jewish?" And
my friend Neil would be like, "Um . . . Yeah?" And my
Grampa'd be like, "Neil, in the year nineteen-twenty-
three I was the greatest Jewish aviator in this country.
That's because I was the *only* Jewish aviator in this country. You wanna see a picture?" And then he would break
out his clippings, which had these photos of himself in his
fuckin' Sopwith Camel that he carried with him *all the
time.* He was pretty amusing.

JESSICA

Is he still alive?

WARREN

Nah, nah . . .

JESSICA

Where does your Mom live?

WARREN

Santa Barbara.

JESSICA

God, so why don't you go stay with her? That's supposed
to be pretty nice.

WARREN

I don't particularly want to live in California, for one thing.

JESSICA

Why not?

WARREN

Because of the *people* in it. Plus my Mom lives with her
boyfriend . . . And anyway, she's kind of freaked out gen-
erally, so it's kind of tough to be around her for very long
at one stretch.

JESSICA

Did you . . . didn't you have a sister that died? Or something?

WARREN

Um . . .

He hesitates for a long moment.

WARREN

. . . Yeah. I did.

JESSICA

So—I mean—is that why you say your Mom, your Mom is
freaked out?

WARREN

I would say it was definitely a prominent factor.

JESSICA

What did your sister die of?

WARREN

Um, she was murdered.

JESSICA

Oh my God, is that true?

WARREN

No, that's just a little joke we have about it in the family.

JESSICA

What?

WARREN

Yeah it's *true*.

JESSICA

I'm sorry: I didn't mean, "Is that true?" I just meant . . .
You know, "Oh my God."

WARREN

Yeah . . .

JESSICA

How did it happen? Do you mind talking about it . . . ?

WARREN

Not really. Do you want any pot?

He picks up the roach.

JESSICA

No, no thanks. But you go ahead.

WARREN

Um— That's all right.

He puts down the roach.

JESSICA

So what happened? That is so horrible.

WARREN

Um, nothing. She was living with this guy named Julian. And my parents were kind of freaked out that she was living with this guy because she was only nineteen, and he was much older. (*Very long pause.*) It's really not my favorite topic.

JESSICA (*Blushing.*)

I'm sorry! . . .

WARREN

That's OK . . .

JESSICA

. . . I'm, sorry . . .

WARREN

It's OK . . .

Long silence. She is very embarrased. He holds out the roach to her.

WARREN

Do you want any of this?

JESSICA

OK.

He lights the roach and gives it to her. She takes a hit, doesn't get much, or coughs, but doesn't relight it or try again. Silence.

JESSICA

The Wild City.

She turns and looks at him thoughtfully for a moment.

JESSICA

Are those your records?

WARREN

Um, yeah. These are my authentic first release Sixties albums, all in perfect condition. Got the whole thing here: Early Mothers, Captain Beefheart, Herman's Hermits, everything. You wanna hear one?

JESSICA

Sure.

He puts on a high-velocity Frank Zappa song, e.g., "Mystery Roach," from 200 Motels.

JESSICA

All *right!*

She nods and starts dancing.

JESSICA

Wake this dump *up!*

WARREN

All right!

WARREN *starts dancing in his own separate space. He takes a few tentative steps toward her, then she moves unambiguously to him, and they start dancing more or less together.*

JESSICA

Uh *huh,* uh *huh,* uh *huh* uh *huh* uh *huh.*

She opens her arms, and WARREN *steps into them. The music abruptly segues into a Zappa-esque confusion of sound that is impossible to dance to.*

WARREN

Um—I don't know. I guess you can't really dance to this next song too well.

JESSICA

Well . . .

WARREN

Hold on.

He hurries to the stereo and puts on a slow, romantic song, e.g., "Lucille," from Joe's Garage Part II.

JESSICA

Oh. OK. Goes for the slow song. I get it.

WARREN

Of course.

JESSICA

OK. I'm game.

She starts to take his hands.

JESSICA

Wait. (*She lets go.*) I've got a hair in my mouth.

She extracts the hair from her mouth, shakes it off her finger, and puts her hands back up. They dance, not entirely gracelessly.

WARREN

I'm definitely into actual dancing.

JESSICA

Yeah, I think our generation definitely missed out in the dancing department.

WARREN

Yeah . . . I guess like, whoever the genius was who decided you didn't need *steps* should have come up with something else instead.

JESSICA

Yeah, right?

He dips her.

JESSICA

Check him *out*. Mr. *Dip*.

He brings her back up again.

JESSICA

You could be a really good dancer.

WARREN

Thanks. So could you. (*A joke:*) If only society would give us a chance.

JESSICA

Yeah, man!

They dance.

WARREN

Listen—

JESSICA

Yeah?

WARREN

I just gotta say, I find you incredibly attractive.

JESSICA

OK— Relax, will you?

WARREN

But listen—would you be mortally offended if I kissed you for just a second?

JESSICA

Well, I mean, what's the rush?

WARREN

No rush. I'd just like to get rid of this knot in my stomach.

JESSICA

Oh— Sure, I mean—whatever's expedient.

WARREN (*Moving closer.*)
No— It's just . . .

JESSICA (*Letting him.*)
Yeah . . . ?

WARREN *kisses her. She kisses back. It quickly turns into heavy teen-age-style making-out.* JESSICA *breaks away.*

JESSICA
They're gonna walk in, and I'm gonna be really embarrassed.

WARREN (*A blatant lie.*)
Yeah—me too.

She takes a few steps away and looks back at him sharply.

JESSICA
They *are* coming back, right?

WARREN
Yeah . . . !

JESSICA
OK. Just checking. (*Pause.*) But I mean . . . do you like me, Warren, or what?

WARREN
Of course I do! Can't you tell?

JESSICA
I don't know. Not really. Maybe you just want to mess around or something.

WARREN
Um, I do. *And* I like you. I completely enjoy talking to you . . .

JESSICA
Well, OK, which would you prefer if you had to choose?

Pause.

WARREN

That would depend on which one we'd already been doing more *of*.

JESSICA

All right. Never mind. Stupid question. I'm sorry. It's just, I'm always getting drawn into these situations and then getting hurt really badly. So . . .

WARREN

Noted.

JESSICA

You wanna close your eyes for a second?

WARREN

Yes.

He closes his eyes. JESSICA *crosses to him and kisses him, until they are both sprawled inelegantly on* DENNIS's *horrible mattress, feeling each other up and getting so worked up that* JESSICA *pulls away again, not out of coquetry but just to put on the brakes.*

JESSICA

OK, gotta take a break.

WARREN

Well . . . I mean—if you want to, we could go someplace else.

JESSICA

What do you mean? Like, to your house or something?

WARREN

Um—no, my house wouldn't work out too well right now . . .

JESSICA

Well, we can't go to *my* house.

WARREN

Well, look, why don't we— Why don't we just go rent the

penthouse suite at the *Plaza* or something, and like hang out and order room service and like watch the sun come up over the park.

JESSICA

How could we do that?

WARREN

Because I happen to be extremely liquid at the moment.

JESSICA

Are you serious?

WARREN

Yeah . . . !

JESSICA

Well . . . what about Dennis and Valerie?

WARREN

I'll leave them a note. Or, we can just tell them where we are, and have them meet us there, or we can just hang out by ourselves. . . . Whatever we feel like doing.

JESSICA

Um—all right.

WARREN

Really?

JESSICA

Sure. I mean . . . yeah.

WARREN

All right. Let me just get some funding.

He goes to the shoe bag and takes out a couple of bricks of cash.

JESSICA

Oh my *God.* Is that *money* in there?

WARREN

I'm afraid so.

JESSICA

Where did you get that?

WARREN

These are the proceeds from my unhappy childhood.

JESSICA

The what . . . ?

WARREN

I'll tell you about it later. Are you ready?

JESSICA

I'm ready.

She slings her purse over her shoulder. Stops.

JESSICA

Shit! I should've called my mother.

WARREN

What for?

JESSICA

I'm just supposed to call her if I'm gonna be out after twelve-thirty.

WARREN

Doesn't that wake her?

JESSICA

She doesn't care, she goes right back to sleep.

WARREN

Do you want to call her now?

JESSICA

No. She's just gonna freak out 'cause I didn't call earlier. I

don't know. I'll just deal with it later ... I don't know why
the fuck she's always so *worried* about me.

They go out.

ACT TWO

The next day, a little after noon. On the little table is a small laboratory scale, a brown paper bag, an unopened jar of Mannitol, a tablespoon, an upside-down porcelain dinner plate, a nearly unfurled ten dollar bill, and a straight-edged razor.

DENNIS *is sprawled out asleep on his mattress in a crazy tangle of sheets, wearing only a T-shirt and a pair of boxer shorts. The buzzer buzzes.* DENNIS *stirs but does not wake. The buzzer buzzes again. He sits up, then staggers to the intercom and presses the Talk button.*

                    DENNIS
    What?

                    WARREN (*On the intercom.*)
    It's Warren.

DENNIS *buzzes him in, unlocks the door and leaves it ajar, then collapses back onto the bed.* WARREN *comes in looking chipper. He carries a small deli bag with a coffee in it.*

                    WARREN
    Hey.

                    DENNIS
    Where've you been? What happened to you?

WARREN

Nothing. I was with Jessica.

DENNIS

You were with her this whole time?

WARREN

Pretty much.

DENNIS

What time is it?

WARREN

Around noon.

DENNIS *goes into the bathroom, leaving the door open. Over the following, we hear him pee and flush the toilet. He comes out.*

WARREN

So . . . Did you get that Z from Stuey?

DENNIS *(Off.)*

Yeah. It's *great*. Me and Valerie were doing lines with him and *Bergita* for like two and a half hours. Plus he says the heroin he has is like really amazing too.

WARREN

Who's Bergita? The Dutch girl?

DENNIS *comes back out.*

DENNIS

Yeah. She was pretty cute. I don't understand how that guy gets girls, man. He is like a classically ugly man.

He collapses on the bed again.

WARREN

Where's Valerie?

DENNIS

Oh, *Valerie*. Valerie walked in here and took one look at the shards of her sculpture lying in the garbage and went completely insane. She was screaming at me so loud it literally hurt my *ears*. She was like, "You're totally selfish, you do whatever you want, you never apologize to anyone, you have no idea how to deal with people, and you're gonna die alone." Then she burst into tears and fled to her aunt's house in Connecticut. I totally blame you.

WARREN

Sorry about that, man.

DENNIS

I don't give a shit. She's out of her mind.

WARREN

So—is this it?

DENNIS

Yeah.

WARREN *picks up a brown paper bag off the table and very carefully takes out of it a double-wrapped ziplock baggy containing an ounce of cocaine.*

WARREN

That's a lot of blow.

DENNIS

Yeah. Now put it down before you break it.

WARREN *puts down the bag of cocaine.*

DENNIS

So what happened with you and that girl?

WARREN

Nothing. I had a nice time.

DENNIS

Did you fuck her?

WARREN

Um . . . Yeah. I did.

DENNIS

You did? As in actual penetration?

WARREN

Basically.

DENNIS

No—what do you mean "basically"? Did you or didn't
you?

WARREN

No—I did.

DENNIS

So that's amazing.

WARREN

I'm pretty pleased.

DENNIS

Warren. Breaks the losing streak.

WARREN

Yeah. I kind of like her. She really likes to argue. But I'm
into that.

DENNIS

So where did you go? Her house?

WARREN

No, man, I took her to the fuckin' Vanderbilt Suite at the
Plaza Hotel.

DENNIS

No you didn't.

WARREN

Yes I did.

DENNIS

You took her to the *Plaza*?

WARREN

Yeah. I got this really beautiful suite, and we just drank champagne and looked out over the park and made love on the *balcony*. It was pretty intense.

Pause.

DENNIS

You should have gone to the Pierre.

WARREN

Why do you say that?

DENNIS

Because the Plaza is a dump. My old man says it used to be amazing, but now it's totally run down and rancid and the Pierre is just a much, much better hotel. You gotta stay at the Pierre or the Carlton or like the Carlyle.

WARREN

Well—I never stayed at any of them, but I definitely thought the Plaza was pretty cool.

DENNIS

So were you actually able to do anything with her? Or did you just like come immediately?

WARREN

I came pretty fast.

DENNIS

Naturally. You only did it once?

WARREN

Well . . . I think she kind of freaked out a little bit afterwards.

DENNIS
What do you mean? What'd she do?

WARREN
Well, she didn't really freak out, but she definitely got pretty quiet. And I was like, "What's the matter? We just had an amazing time together, and I really like you." And she was like, "But I don't even *know* you." So I was like, "Well you know me now." But I don't really know if she agreed with that interpretation.

DENNIS *crosses to the table and starts opening up the bag of cocaine to show* WARREN.

DENNIS
Yeah. Don't worry about that. A lot of times your average girl teen will bug out immediately following a swift and manly conquest. It's no big deal. You didn't do anything to her that she didn't do to you. Just call her up and, you know, take her to the *zoo* or something. Only don't sit here and start getting depressed after you finally got laid with a completely good-looking girl after a *drought* like the fucking Irish *potato* famine of *eighteen-forty-eight*, because you're bringing me down. You should be totally proud of yourself and not get into your usual self-flagellating stew just because you came too fast and she freaked out afterwards. (*He laughs.*) Now come here and look at the crystal formation on this rock. It's unbelievable.

WARREN *looks*.

WARREN
That's a big rock.

DENNIS
It's a big rock. This baby alone would probably pay for your whole *night* at the Plaza. You know?

WARREN
I doubt it.

DENNIS

Why? How much did you spend?

WARREN

I guess it was around a thousand bills all told, but I didn't really tally it up yet.

DENNIS

You spent a *thousand dollars* on that girl when she was totally ready to fuck you for free?

WARREN

I wasn't so sure, man. She seemed kinda skittish.

DENNIS

So, what, now you're in the hole for twenty-five hundred bucks?

WARREN

Twenty-seven.

DENNIS

What is the *matter* with you? How did you spend that much *money*?

WARREN

I'm not really sure.

DENNIS

OK: You're outta control. You are like hell bent for destruction and I want nothing more to fuckin' *do* with it! I can't sell twenty-seven hundred dollars worth of blow before tomorrow *morning*.

WARREN

Why not?

DENNIS

Because it's totally *impossible*! I'll make the *calls*, but I can't speed the natural pace of the market. It's just not gonna happen. Besides, your share of the profits only comes to thirteen hundred minus my fuckin' service fee! And even if it *didn't*, I'm not letting you stay here all week with that money, Warren, because when your father finds out you spent that money on drugs, he's gonna think I'm in *cahoots* with you, and then he's gonna forgive *you* and kill *me*.

> WARREN

No he's not.

> DENNIS

Yes he is! How could you spend another thousand dollars?!

> WARREN

It was surprisingly easy.

> DENNIS

All right: That's it. Get on the phone, call Christian, tell him we need distribution help. Tell him you'll give him whatever he wants out of your half and if he can't help us move all 20 grams by tonight you're comin' over there to stay with *him*. Because I am officially closing the Dennis Ziegler Home For Runaway Boys. You understand me?

> WARREN

Who am I calling? Christian?

> DENNIS

Yeah, Christian!

> WARREN

All right . . . !

As WARREN *picks up the phone,* DENNIS *roams around the room.*

> DENNIS

Oh you are so stupid, man. You are so stupid. If your father finds you here, man, he's gonna sic that fuckin' *driver* on me and I am totally gonna have to leave town. And this is such a bad time for me.

WARREN (*Holding the phone*)
Did you have breakfast yet?

DENNIS
No I didn't have breakfast. I just got up.

WARREN
Let's take a run over to Zabars and pick up a smoked salmon.

DENNIS
DIAL THE PHONE!

WARREN *dials the phone.*

WARREN (*Into the phone.*)
Hello Mr. Berkman, is Christian there? . . . Oh, OK. Could you please tell him that Warren Straub called? . . . I'm fine, how are you? . . . Not too much. How's *Mrs.* Berkman?

DENNIS
GET OFF THE PHONE!

WARREN (*Into the phone.*)
Anyway—could you just tell him I called, and he can call me at Dennis Ziegler's house?

DENNIS *makes a wild, negative, cut-off gesture.*

WARREN
Actually, just tell him I'll try him later . . . Thanks a lot.

He hangs up.

DENNIS
What's the *matter* with you?

WARREN
Nothing. Why don't you calm down?

DENNIS

Oh you are really asking for it. Maybe I can get ahold of
Philip.

The phone rings. They look at it fearfully. It keeps ringing. DENNIS
picks it up tentatively.

DENNIS (*Into the phone*)
Yeah? . . . BECAUSE *I* DIDN'T *BREAK* YOUR
FUCKIN' SCULPTURE, *WARREN* BROKE IT!

*He slams the phone down as hard as he possibly can. Runs his raging
fingers through his hair.*

WARREN (*Starts to speak.*)

DENNIS *grabs the phone and dials furiously. Waits.*

DENNIS (*Into the phone.*)
I just want you to think about what a sick, unhappy person
you are that after all the serious problems we've been having for the last three months over your relentless *identity*
crisis—*which has nothing to fuckin' do with me!*—we're
finally getting along together like we fuckin' love each
other, and you freak out at me *this much* and get me *this
angry* at you, because one of my *friends* accidentally broke
your semi-Lesbian progressive-school clay *sculpture*! . . .
It was on the *shelf* so I could *look* at it! Will you *listen*
to yourself? Will you listen to what you're *saying*? . . .
YOU TORTURE ME ABOUT A *SCULPTURE*, YOU
PSYCHOTIC MONSTER!? I'D LIKE TO RIP YOUR
FUCKIN' HEAD OFF!

He slams the phone down and kicks it as hard as he can across the room.

WARREN
You have a nice touch, man.

DENNIS
Shut up! (*He starts laughing.*) I'm sick, *sick*! All right:
Christian's not home and I ain't callin' Philip. What about
this shit? Could you sell any of this?

He rattles WARREN'*s open suitcase full of toys.*

> WARREN
>
> Um—yeah. I can sell *all* of it.

> DENNIS
>
> Really? For how much? Could you get two thousand dollars for what's in here?

> WARREN
>
> I don't know. I never really tallied it up, but I'm fairly sure I could get considerably *more* than that.

> DENNIS
>
> Oh, we are selling this *today*. I'm calling Adam Saulk's brother right now.

He picks up the phone. Stops.

> DENNIS
>
> Is that OK?

> WARREN
>
> Go ahead.

DENNIS *dials the phone.*

> DENNIS
>
> All right. Maybe this'll solve everything. (*Into the phone.*) Is that Donald? . . . Dennis Ziegler, man, what's goin' on? . . . I'm all right. Listen, do you know Warren *Straub*? . . . Yeah. So he's got like a lot of really high quality toys and shit from like the Fifties and Sixties, and about thirty really rare first-release albums—(*Covers the phone. To* WARREN, *who is signalling him.*) What?

> WARREN
>
> I think you should mention the toaster.

> DENNIS
>
> No, he doesn't care about your *toaster*, Warren. (*Into the phone.*) One second, man.

WARREN

Yes he does. It's really rare.

DENNIS (*Covers the phone.*)

It's worth money?

WARREN

Yeah.

DENNIS (*Into the phone.*)

Sorry, man—he's also got this incredibly rare toaster from like . . . *eighteen-forty-seven.*

WARREN

Nineteen-fifty-five.

DENNIS (*Into the phone.*)
From *nineteen-fifty-five.* Like a completely rare edition of toaster. I'm not sure what the actual model is, but—I said I'm not sure what the actual model is, but I definitely know it is one fine toaster. (*Covers the phone.*) Would you shut up!

WARREN
Tell him they recalled it.

Tell him they recalled it.

D. Tell him they recalled it.

WARREN *shuts up.*

DENNIS (*Into the phone*)

Yeah, man—anyway—he was gonna sell some of this shit to his regular boy, but I told him I had a friend who could probably come up with a much better price, and I wanted to try to give you the business if you were interested. But the thing is, Donald? Donald? This stuff is like really good, so I don't wanna waste my time if you're not totally prepared to step up to the plate. You know what I mean there, Donald? . . . Yeah?. . . All right . . . No, this afternoon's not so good for me, man: I'm going to a ball game with my brother . . . No, man, Warren's like ready to *go* . . . Well what are you doing right now? . . . All right, gimme

your address. (*Writes down the address.*) All right, man,
see you in a few.

He hangs up.

DENNIS

I am a total business *genius*. I don't even know what this
shit is *worth* and I'm already getting you like the best possible price for it. I am just like completely naturally gifted
at business.

WARREN

Well . . . There is my usual guy, who's definitely offered me
decent money for the whole collection at various times,
so—

DENNIS

No, never mind your usual *guy*. You should totally let me
handle this transaction for you, Warren, because this guy
is like completely intimidated by me, and I'm just gonna
get you much more money. All right?

WARREN

Whatever.

DENNIS

All right. Now before I go over there, tell me what would
be the best possible money you could *possibly* get for this
shit.

WARREN

I don't know. If you include the records, I guess the best
price you could hope to get would be like, I don't know,
like *maybe* twenty-five at the very outside.

DENNIS

You're seriously telling me this *junk* is worth twenty-five
hundred bucks?

WARREN

Yeah. Because it's a really good collection. But you probably won't get that.

DENNIS

All right. Now listen to me, Warren. I am not selling your *baby* toys if you don't tell me it's OK, because I don't want you *guilting* it over my head for the rest of my life. OK? But if you don't want me to, I am totally throwing you out of here right now. Because I have no desire to incur the Wrath of Jason, and you can't just walk in here and dump your *situation* on me and then obstruct every possible solution I come up with just because you're a destructive little *freak* who has to like *wreck* everything so you can get everybody whipped into a *frenzy* over you all the time. But I don't want you telling me later that I forced you into selling your precious belongings, because it's totally up to *you*. All right?

WARREN

No. Go ahead and sell 'em. I don't know what else to do.

DENNIS *starts getting dressed.*

DENNIS

All right. If this stuff is worth twenty-five bills then I probably won't have to sell *all* of it, so tell me which of these I should try to hang onto and which I should immediately toss into the gaping maw of Donald Saulk.

WARREN

I guess . . . save the Major Matt Masons for last . . . And if you can, I guess I'd prefer it if you didn't sell the toaster.

Pause.

DENNIS

I just totally humiliated myself talking up this fuckin' toaster, now you're telling me I can't *sell* it?

WARREN

Not if you don't have to, no. I don't know how much he's gonna offer—

DENNIS

All right. I'll try.

WARREN

And give me the hat.

DENNIS *picks up the baseball cap.*

DENNIS

We can't sell this?

WARREN

I don't think so.

DENNIS

Why not? You could get money for this, couldn't you?

WARREN

I know I could, but I'm not selling it.

DENNIS

All right.

DENNIS *gives* WARREN *the baseball cap and starts packing up the suitcase.*

The buzzer buzzes.

DENNIS

It's Jason!

WARREN

It's not Jason!

DENNIS

It's totally Jason! I'm going across the roof!

WARREN

It's not Jason, he doesn't even know I'm here!

DENNIS
He knows who your *friends* are! You think he didn't. figure out where you *went*? You only *have* two friends! All right!

WARREN
But it's not him, you fuckin' *socio*path: he's throwing a *brunch*!

Pause.

DENNIS
You answer it.

WARREN
No way.

DENNIS
Why not?

WARREN
Because it's not my house, man.

DENNIS
So what?

WARREN
I don't wanna answer it. What if it's him?

DENNIS
All right. Shut up.

WARREN
I wasn't talking.

DENNIS
Shut *up*!

DENNIS *goes to the intercom and hits the Talk button.*

DENNIS
Yeah?

JESSICA (*On the intercom.*)
It's Jessica Goldman. Is Warren there?

DENNIS (*To* WARREN.)
I'm gonna *kill* you, Warren.

WARREN
I didn't know she was coming here.

DENNIS
That scared the shit out of me.

WARREN
Why? Just buzz her in.

DENNIS *hits the buzzer and goes to the suitcase.*

DENNIS
All right. Saulk's only on Eighty-First, so I won't be long.
I'll do my best, and I'll try to save Major Matt Mason if I
can. But he might be called upon to make the ultimate
Outer Space sacrifice.

WARREN
I understand, man . . . Farewell, Toaster Amazing.

WARREN *unhappily watches* DENNIS *pack away the last of the collection and zip up the suitcase.*

DENNIS
All right. Cheer up, man. Your troubles are almost over.

WARREN
I'm cheerful.

There is a knock on the door. DENNIS *is nearest the door and opens it.*
JESSICA *stands in* the doorway.

JESSICA
Hi, Dennis. How are you?

DENNIS
I'm fine, Jessica. How are *you*?

JESSICA
Fine.

DENNIS
Are you from the Leg Embassy?

He is referring to her short skirt.

JESSICA
Yeah, I'm the Ambassador.

DENNIS
Stay with it.

JESSICA *comes into the room.*

JESSICA (*To* WARREN.)
Hey. I was just around the corner so I thought I'd buzz up.

WARREN (*Bizarrely, to* JESSICA.)
Good Morgen to all good Norsemen.

JESSICA
Excuse me?

WARREN
How many Norse Horsemen does it take to Smoke a Herring?

DENNIS *laughs rudely and loudly at* WARREN*'s awkward attempt at eccentric humor and goes into the bathroom, closing the door behind him. We hear the sink running.* WARREN *crosses with awkward confidence toward* JESSICA.

WARREN
All Norse Horsemen smoke Morgen Cigarettes.

JESSICA
Am I supposed to know what you're talking about?

WARREN
I'm not talking about anything. It's just something to say.
Don't you want to kiss me Good Morgen?

He comes to her to kiss her. It doesn't go too well. She turns her face or ducks her head so he can't kiss her.

JESSICA (*Low, referring to* DENNIS *in the bathroom.*)
Um, can we please not, like . . .

WARREN
Sorry.

JESSICA
That's OK . . .

She moves away from him. DENNIS *comes out of the bathroom. He sits on the floor to put on his sneakers.*

WARREN
So D. How long you think you're gonna be?

DENNIS (*Looking at* JESSICA.)
I don't know. How much time do you need?

WARREN (*Confused.*)
Um . . . We were gonna get some food . . .

JESSICA
How much *time* do we need?

DENNIS (*To* WARREN.)
So who's stoppin' you?

WARREN
I was actually wondering about the *key*.

JESSICA (*To* DENNIS.)
How much time do we need for *what*?

DENNIS
For whatever dastardly deed you're planning to *indulge* in, Jessica.

JESSICA
I don't think we're gonna be indulging in anything very dastardly, to tell you the truth, Dennis.

WARREN
I thought we were gonna be indulging in some *brunch*.

DENNIS
So *that's* your story, eh? (*A la Snidely Whiplash.*) Yeh heh heh heh . . . !

JESSICA
What is he *talking* about?

WARREN
Denny, man, you're my *best friend*.

DENNIS (*Getting up.*)
All right, kids, I'm outta here. Try to find some way to entertain yourselves.

JESSICA
Don't leave on my account.

DENNIS
Don't worry about it. (*To* WARREN.) Be back in a half.

DENNIS *exits, with the suitcase.*

JESSICA
Where's he going?

WARREN
He just has a business transaction to perform.

JESSICA

What is he, like the big drug dealer or something?

WARREN

He's the big everything.

JESSICA

Well . . . Sorry to bust in on you like this—

WARREN

That's OK.

JESSICA

—but I actually just wanted to tell you I can't have brunch.

WARREN

Why not?

JESSICA

Well, when I got home this morning I had this really huge fight with my Mom and I think I'd better just be at home today. She kind of freaked out that I never called last night, so now she wants to have some big landmark discussion about how we're gonna handle my living there this year . . .

WARREN

Well . . . Thanks for cancelling in person.

JESSICA

Well, I'm sorry, but my Mom is really upset and getting along with her is a really big priority for me right now. I tried to call before, but the line was busy.

WARREN

Do you want to make a plan for any time this week?

JESSICA

I think I'd better just chill out a little bit this week, actually.

WARREN

All right.

Silence.

JESSICA

Well . . . You seem like you're really angry . . .

WARREN

I'm not.

JESSICA

Well, that's not the impression you're *conveying*, but . . .

WARREN

No—I guess I just don't understand why you walked ten blocks out of your way so you could be around the corner so you could buzz up and tell me you can't have brunch with me.

JESSICA

Uh, no: I told you I tried to call . . .

WARREN

Yeah—he was on the phone for like two *minutes*.

JESSICA

All right, I'm *sorry*.

WARREN

There's nothing to be sorry about.

JESSICA

All right.

She goes slowly to the door and puts her hand on the knob.

JESSICA

So . . . can I ask you something?

WARREN

Go ahead.

JESSICA

Did you tell Dennis what happened last night?

Pause.

WARREN

Um . . . I guess.

JESSICA

Really. What did you say?

WARREN

Nothing. I said we had a nice time.

JESSICA

That's all?

WARREN

Pretty much.

JESSICA

I find that really hard to believe.

WARREN

Why?

JESSICA

I don't know. Don't you guys get into like comparing *notes* and stuff?

WARREN

I'm not really into that.

JESSICA

Well . . . OK . . . It's just— This is getting a little weird now, because when I talked to Valerie, she asked *me* if anything happened with us last night. And for some reason, I guess I didn't really tell her that anything did. So now she's gonna talk to *Dennis*, and I'm gonna look like a total *liar* to someone I'm just starting to be close friends with and who I really care about . . . !

WARREN

Um . . . So . . . I don't really get . . . You're mad at me because you lied to Valerie?

JESSICA

No . . . I just should have figured that you would like rush off to tell your friends that you *fucked* me—

WARREN

Whoa!

JESSICA

—whereas I might be more inclined to be a little more *discreet* about it till I found out where I stood with you.

WARREN

I didn't fuckin' rush off *any*where!

JESSICA

Yeah, whatever, you know what? It doesn't matter—

WARREN

I came *back* here 'cause I'm *staying* here—

JESSICA

OK, but you know what? It really doesn't matter—

WARREN

And the minute I walked in he like totally *grilled* me—

JESSICA

Oh so you just tell him whatever he wants to know no matter what the consequences are for somebody else?

WARREN

No! Will you let me finish my—

JESSICA (*On "Let."*)

But honestly, Warren? I really don't care who you told, or what you told them, because people are gonna think whatever they think and you know what? There's nothing I can do about it.

WARREN

What people? What are you talking about!

JESSICA

I don't know, but whatever it is I must be wrong because of the way you're *yelling*.

WARREN

You're not anything!

JESSICA

Well, it really—I should just really listen to my instincts, you know? Because your instincts are never wrong. And it was totally against my instinct to come over here last night, and it was definitely against my instinct to *sleep* with you, but I did and it's too late. And now my Mom is totally furious at me, I probably ruined my friendship with Valerie, and now like Dennis *Ziegler* thinks I'm like, easy *pickins*, or something—

WARREN

Nobody thinks anything—

JESSICA

And it's not like I even care what he thinks, OK? Because I don't actually *know* him. Or you. Or *Valerie*, for that matter! So it doesn't really matter! I've made new friends before, I can make more new friends now if I have to. So let's just forget the whole thing ever happened, you can chalk one up in your *book*, or whatever—

WARREN

I don't *have* a *book*.

JESSICA
—and I'll just *know* better next time! Hopefully. OK?

Pause.

WARREN
I don't really get what you're so upset about.

JESSICA
Well: I guess I'm just *insane.*

WARREN
I thought we had a really good time together, and I was actually in a fairly *up* state of mind for once.

JESSICA
I'm sure you were.

WARREN
Well, I didn't mean that in any kind of lascivious way, so I don't know why you want to take it like that. I really like you.

JESSICA
Yeah, whatever.

WARREN
No not whatever! I'm sorry I said anything to Dennis. I definitely caved in to the peer pressure. But I also definitely said as little as possible and was totally respectful of you in the way I talked about you. Even though I was pretty excited about what happened last night, and also about like, maybe like, the prospect of like, I don't know, like, going *out* with you—which I would be very into, if you were. But if you want to think the whole thing meant nothing to me, then go ahead, because that's not the case.

JESSICA
Well . . . You know, I really—

WARREN

It's totally weird, like taking all your clothes off and having sex with someone you barely know, and then being like, "What's up *now*?" You know? Like it's such an intense experience, but then nobody knows what to fuckin' say, even though nothing really bad actually happened. You know?

JESSICA

. . . Well . . . I don't know . . .

WARREN

But I really like you . . . I don't really agree with most of your *opinions* . . .

JESSICA

Oh, thank you.

WARREN

. . . but I don't meet a lot of people who can actually make me *think*, you know? And who can hold their own in an interesting discussion. And who I'm totally hot for at the same time. You know? It's a fairly effective combination.

Pause.

JESSICA

I don't know, Warren. Things are just really weird in my life right now. And everything you're saying is really sweet, but I have literally no idea whether you mean it or not. It's like my instinct is just *broken* . . . And I guess sometimes actions speak louder than words . . .

WARREN

But what action could I possibly take except to say I'm sorry for whatever it is you think I've done?

JESSICA (*A joke.*)

Presents are always nice. Just kidding.

                              WARREN
          You want a present?

                              JESSICA
          I'm just kidding.

                              WARREN
          Why? I'm sitting on twelve thousand *dollars.* I'll buy you a
          sports car. OK?

                              JESSICA
          That's OK. I don't have a license yet.

                              WARREN
          Well, what do you want?

Pause.

                              JESSICA
            . . . Are you serious?

                              WARREN
          Name it.

                              JESSICA
          OK . . . (*Pause.*) Um . . . Could I have the hat?

Pause.

                              WARREN
          Definitely.

Pause.

                              JESSICA
          Really?

                              WARREN
          It's yours.

He picks up the baseball cap and holds it out to her.

WARREN

Here.

Pause. JESSICA *looks at him uncertainly.*

JESSICA

. . . Don't if you don't want to.

WARREN

I really want to.

JESSICA

Why?

WARREN

Because I really like you.

Pause. She reaches out slowly and takes the hat.

JESSICA

Well—I don't know what to say . . .

WARREN *does not respond.*

JESSICA

I mean—I can't believe it . . . ! I can't believe that you would give me something that means this much to you— I don't even know what to say.

WARREN

Good.

She puts it on her head and self-consciously "models" it for him.

JESSICA

What do you think?

WARREN

. . . Looks great on you . . .

JESSICA

You think?

WARREN

Definitely.

She looks at him. He is clearly in distress and can't hide it.

JESSICA

Well, you look totally miserable.

WARREN

I'm not.

She takes off the hat.

JESSICA

Well I'm sorry, but I feel really weird taking your grandfather's hat.

WARREN

Then why'd you fucking ask me for it?

JESSICA *flushes a deep mortified red.*

JESSICA
I was *totally kidding*
when I asked you for
something—

WARREN
No you weren't!

JESSICA

—Yes I was! But then you *insisted* I pick something! Only why did you *give* it me if you don't want me to *have* it?

WARREN

Because I really want you to have it!

JESSICA

But why do you keep *saying* that when you obviously DON'T?

WARREN

NO! God *damn*! What do I have to do, like BEG you to take it from me?

A long moment.

JESSICA

OK. Sorry.

She puts the hat back on her head. Silence.

JESSICA

Well . . . I mean . . . Should I just go home?

WARREN (*Looking at the floor*)

I don't know . . . Do whatever.

JESSICA

Well, then I guess I will.

She goes to the door.

JESSICA

Should I assume you no longer want to go out this week?

WARREN

I don't think we can. I'm all out of baseball hats.

JESSICA *takes off the hat.*

JESSICA

Can I please say something?

WARREN

You try to give me that hat back one more time, I swear to
God I'll fuckin' *burn* it . . . !

Pause. JESSICA *puts the baseball cap down on the table.*

JESSICA

Well . . . That would be up to you.

She turns and exits. WARREN *sits very still for a minute. Then he gets
up and carefully puts the hat away with his stuff. He sits at the table
and carefully dumps all the cocaine on the dinner plate and looks at it.*

He spoons some Mannitol onto the plate, and starts mixing the two powders together, concentrating intensely.

The phone rings. He reaches for it and knocks the entire plate of cocaine onto the floor. He doesn't know what to do for a minute. He laughs. The phone keeps ringing. He answers it.

WARREN *(Into the phone.)*
Hello?

He stands up like he just got an electric shock. He listens for a moment.

WARREN
Well, Dad, I guess the jig is up . . . W— Well I— Could I— I was planning on *returning* it . . . Thank you . . . Well, you're actually gonna have to wait like an hour . . . Do whatever you want, but I won't be here . . . Why don't you punch me in the face and throw me out of the apartment? . . . That is definitely my intention . . . Uh huh . . . I don't know, Dad: What kind of world do *you* think I'm living in? . . .

Pause. He sits down. More quietly:

WARREN
Yeah. I think about her all the time . . . I don't really know, Dad. I just see her in my imagination, I guess . . . Well, I feel pretty strongly about the fact that I have a lot better judgment than she did at my age, and it's also not too likely that I'm gonna move in with some thirty-five year-old guy who beats me up all the time. So I don't really think it's an appropriate comparison. Although I will say that it's a totally obvious one. By which I mean I don't think it's all that clever . . . All right: I know your brunching companions await . . . Well, it is really hard to fully appreciate what your girlfriend has to go through, but it's really fucking fortunate that she has both the good looks and the intelligence to see her through all the rough spots . . . Sounds good . . . Do whatever you want . . . I hate you too.

His father hangs up. WARREN *hangs up too.*

He looks at the cocaine on the floor. He starts to scrape what he can off the floor and onto the plate. But it's an impossible job. He suddenly stomps on the cocaine, smearing it all over the floor with wild kicks. After a moment of this, he stops.

DENNIS *comes in, very freaked out. He puts down the suitcase, now empty.*

DENNIS

What are you doing? What happened?

WARREN

I knocked the drugs on the floor.

DENNIS

You did *what*?

WARREN

I was trying to mix in the cut.

DENNIS

What? How bad is it?

WARREN

It's pretty bad.

DENNIS

Oh—GOD! OK— All right—I can't even deal with this right now— Listen to me, Warren. Something terrible has happened.

WARREN

What's the matter? Somebody's dead?

DENNIS

Yeah.

WARREN

Who, my mother?

DENNIS (*Furious.*)

No, not your fuckin' *mother*, you idiot—

> WARREN

OK—

> DENNIS

It's *Stuey*.

> WARREN

Who?

> DENNIS

Stuey! Stuey! It's fuckin' Stuey!

> WARREN

Stuey who?

> DENNIS

Stuart! The Fat Man. Stuart Grossbart. What's the matter with you?

> WARREN

Oh shit. *That* Stuey.

> DENNIS

Yeah "that Stuey!" How many fuckin' Stueys do you know?

> WARREN

All right! I couldn't place the name for a second! What happened to him?

> DENNIS

I don't know, man. I guess he did too many speedballs. He was with that Dutch chick all night, and they went to sleep and when she woke up this morning she couldn't wake him up, so she turned him over and there was blood coming out of his nose and his *eyes*, and he was dead.

> WARREN

Whoa.

> DENNIS

I mean I just *saw* the guy last *night*. I am so freaked out. I can't even believe it.

WARREN

How did you find out about it?

DENNIS

'Cause when I got to Donald Saulk's house he was on the phone with Yoffie. So I got on the phone and Yoffie told me he went over to Stuey's this morning and there were all these cops there, and that girl was sitting there freaked out of her mind crying and screaming and like smoking cigarettes and talking half in English and half in Dutch, and Yoffie told the cops he was Stuey's friend and they told him what happened.

WARREN

Stuey.

DENNIS

I guess it's a good thing we didn't do any speedballs. You know?

WARREN

But did we buy bad shit, or what?

DENNIS

I don't think so. I was doing it all night and I didn't wake up with fuckin' blood coming out of *my* nose. Did you?

WARREN

No. But I didn't do any of it yet.

DENNIS

And the *girl* was OK. So I guess he just overdid it. But I am so freaked out. I mean the guy is *dead.* Do you know what that *means*? It's like, he's not gonna be *around* any more, like at *all.* And it's just got me really fuckin' scared. I mean we are such assholes to be doing all this shit, man. At some point in the near future, I am totally stopping. I know he was a big fat slob who totally overdid everything and all he ever ate was like sirloin drenched in butter and sour cream, but the guy was like twenty-three years old and now he's just *gone.* You know? Like he is no more.

WARREN

Yeah.

DENNIS

I don't know, man. I guess there's only a certain amount of time you can keep doing this shit before shit starts to happen to you. I mean I am really scared.

WARREN

So did you sell my stuff?

DENNIS

Yeah.

WARREN

Did you have to sell everything?

DENNIS

Oh yeah.

WARREN

How much did you get for it?

DENNIS

I only got nine hundred.

WARREN

What do you mean?!

DENNIS

I mean you had a totally inflated idea of what that shit was worth, so don't make me feel *bad* about it—

WARREN

I know exactly what it was worth and that guy just *rooked* you.

DENNIS *turns white with rage.*

DENNIS

I am really gonna fuckin' hit you, man! I totally got the best possible deal I could!

WARREN
Then you shouldn't have sold it!

DENNIS
You told me to sell it! At least I didn't knock the fuckin'
coke on the floor, so don't make me feel *bad* about this,
man, all right? I'm freaked out of my mind. So maybe I
didn't do so well. I don't know. I'm sorry. It's better than
nothing.

WARREN
I guess.

Silence.

DENNIS
What happened to that girl?

WARREN
She left.

DENNIS
You already had a fight with her?

WARREN
I'm not really sure what happened.

DENNIS
How could you mess that up so fast? What kind of talent
for misery do you have, man?

WARREN
I don't know. I guess I'm pretty advanced.

DENNIS
Did my girlfriend call back?

WARREN
No.

DENNIS

I think I went too far with her before. But I can't even deal
with it right now. I'm too freaked out.

DENNIS *lies down on his back.*

DENNIS

I just can't believe this, man, it's like so completely bizarre.
And it's not like I even liked the guy that much, you know?
I just *knew* him. You know? But if we had been doing
those speedballs last night we could both be *dead* now. Do
you understand how *close* that is? I mean . . . It's *death.*
Death. It's so incredibly heavy, it's like so much heavier
than like ninety-five percent of the shit you deal with in
the average day that constitutes your supposed life, and it's
like so totally off to the *side* it's like completely ridiculous.
I mean that was *it*. That was his *life*. Period. The Life of
Stuart. A fat Jew from Long Island with a grotesque
accent who sold drugs and ate steak and did nothing of
note like whatsoever. (*He gets up and starts moving
around.*) I don't know, man. I'm like, high on fear. I feel
totally high on fear. I'm like—I don't even know what to
do with myself. I wanna like go to *cooking* school in
Florence, or like go into *show* business. I could so totally be
a completely great chef it's like ridiculous. Or like an actor
or like a director. I should totally direct movies, man, I'd
be a genius at it. Like if you take the average person with
the average sensibility or sense of humor or the way they
look at the world and what thoughts they have or what
they think, and you compare it to the way *I* look at shit and
the shit I come up with to say, or just the *slant* I put on
shit, there's just like no comparison at all. I could totally
make movies, man, I would be like one of the greatest
movie makers of all time. Plus I am like so much better at
sports than anyone I know except Wally and those big
black basketball players, man, but I totally played with
those guys and completely earned their respect, and Wally
was like, "Denny, man, you are the only white friend I
have who I can take uptown and hang out with my friends
and not be *embarrassed*." Because I just go up there and
hang out with them and like get them so much more

stoned than they've ever been in their *life* and like am completely not intimidated by them at all. You know?

WARREN

Yeah.

DENNIS

I'm high on fear, man. I am completely stoned out of my mind on fear. And like you guys think I'm like totally confident and on top of it, but it's not true at all. My fuckin' mother is so fuckin' harsh and wildly extreme that I just got trained to snap back twice as hard the minute anybody starts to fuck with me. That's how I fight with Valerie. Like the minute we get into an argument whatever she says to me I just double it and totally get in her face until she backs down or like has to like, leave the *room*. And it completely works too, because I don't have to take any of the shit I see all my male friends taking from their fuckin' girlfriends, or like the shit my father takes from my mother. I mean all he does is fuckin' lord it over everybody man, over all my brothers and sisters and like all his fuckin' assistants and his dealers and agents and like all these celebrities who buy his art, because he totally knows that he's like a complete living genius and so he's like, "Why should I spend two minutes talking to anybody I don't *want* to?" Except now he's like torturing everyone constantly because he basically never doesn't have to pee, and my mother is freaking out because she's working fourteen hours a day because they cut the money out of all her programs and she's totally predicting major inner city catastrophe in years to come, and she completely has his balls in a vice. She's like, "Eddie, you're an asshole. Eddie, nobody gives a shit if you have to pee: You always have to pee, so shut up." She just *tramples* him, man. She's like, "No matter what you do it doesn't matter, because all you do is sell a bunch of paintings to like, one percent of the population and I'm out there every day like, saving children's *lives* and trying to help real people who are being destroyed by Ronald *Reagan*—So whatever you do and however famous you are it's just a total tissue of conceit, because it's got nothing to do with anybody but rich peo-

ple." She just makes total emasculated mincemeat out of
him and the only thing he can do to fight back is go fuck
some twenty-year-old groupie, only now he can't do that
anymore because he's so sick, so he's just totally in her
power, and all he can do is torture her from like a totally
weaker position, and she's like laughing in his face. My
family is sick, man, they're *sick*. You think your fuckin'
father is crazy? What if like everywhere he went total
strangers like worshipped him as a *god*? Wait till his *health*
starts to go. Can you imagine what that's like? Like seriously, what does that *feel* like, to be looking ahead like five
years and not knowing whether you're still gonna *be* here?
You can totally see why people are religious, man. I mean
how much better would it be to think you're gonna be
*some*where, you know? Instead of absolutely nowhere.
Like *gone*, forever. (*Pause.*) That is so fuckin' scary. I am
so fuckin' scared right now. (*Pause.*) I gotta call my girlfriend. You have totally fucked me up, by the way! How
emblematic of your personality is it that you walk into a
room for *ten minutes* and break the *exact item* calculated
to wreak the maximum possible amount of havoc, no matter where you are? You're a total troublemaker, Warren. I
should totally ban you from my house. I am so keyed up.
I can't shut up. I wish Valerie was here. Maybe I should
call that girl Natalie and see if she'll come over and give
me a blowjob. She really likes me, man. She told my sister
I had beautiful eyes. (*Pause.*) I do have totally amazing
eyes. They're a completely amazing, unique shape. Like
most people with my kind of eyes aren't shaped like this at
all. My eyes are like totally intense and direct. Like if I
look people in the eye, like nine out of ten people can't
even hold my *gaze*. Did you do any of that coke?

WARREN

Not yet.

DENNIS

I don't even want to look at it, man. I'm so freaked out. I
totally feel like donating it to *charity* or something . . . That
is so not funny . . . I wonder if anybody told his family.

WARREN

I'm sure they did.

DENNIS

I wonder if they'll have a funeral.

WARREN

I'm sure they will.

DENNIS

That's gonna be one big casket. I wonder if anybody'll show up.

WARREN

Why wouldn't they?

DENNIS

Because nobody *liked* the guy! I called like six people, and I was so freaked out, and nobody cared at all. They were all like, "Wow. That's amazing. Is the coke all right?" Now, I don't know if that means they're all like totally callous and unfeeling or whether the guy was just a totally reprehensible human being.

WARREN

Well, he didn't really leave me with any lastingly warm impression. I mean, I'm sorry he's dead, but I read the *newspaper* this morning, too, you know?

DENNIS

Well, all I know is if *I* had a fuckin' funeral, there wouldn't be room to *sit*. Someday I'm gonna make a movie about all of us, man. Like if you made that guy Donald Saulk a character in a movie, with all that shit in his apartment, how heavy would that be? And most people would like find some bad fuckin' actor to like do some caricature sitcom imitation of this guy and totally miss all the intense subtleties and qualities of his personality, and if it was me I would just go in there and use the real *guy*, and it would be so much heavier, and so much funnier. Don't you think?

WARREN

I don't know.

DENNIS

But don't you think I would be like an amazing director?

WARREN

I have no idea, man.

Pause.

DENNIS

What do you mean you have no idea?

WARREN

I mean I have no idea.

Pause.

DENNIS

Well I totally would be. I would totally—

WARREN

But you've never *done* it.

DENNIS

What do you mean?

WARREN

I mean you don't know anything *about* it. You just like movies. And have an interest in people's personalities.

DENNIS

No I don't "just like movies." I totally—

WARREN (*On the second "I."*)

I like them too. But I don't necessarily think you'd be a good movie director, because I have no idea if you have the slightest talent for it whatsoever. I'm sorry.

DENNIS

You are really pissing me off.

WARREN

I don't really give a shit, man. Why did you sell my fuckin' toy collection for nine hundred dollars?

DENNIS

Is that what you're mad about? With poor Stuey moldering in the ground?

WARREN

I don't give a fuck about Stuey, and neither do you. I didn't even *know* him.

DENNIS

So call the guy up and get it back and dig your own fuckin' grave, you little asshole! I am totally sick of you and your moronic fuckin' self-imposed *dilemma*! I've been dealing drugs for five years and I never once dropped any of it on the fucking *floor*! Because I am not an *imbecile*! I cannot believe that you do that, and then you have the nerve to give me shit because I undersold your little *toy* box!

Pause.

WARREN

Why do you have to talk to me that way, man?

DENNIS

Why do I talk to you what way?

WARREN

Why do you have to call me an asshole every five seconds? I don't like it.

DENNIS

What do you mean? We call each other shit all the time. Don't start with me, Warren, because all I've been doing for the last two days is like totally try to help you!

WARREN

I know you're doing *something*, man. But I can barely tell if you're even on my side.

DENNIS

What are you *talking* about? I'm on your side, I'm totally on your side.

WARREN

Then why are you always like, reminding me that I haven't done well with girls for a really long time, man?

DENNIS

Because—

WARREN

And like constantly insulting me and like *teasing* me and like telling me how incompetent I am and what a fuck-up I am, like this running motif like *every time* we hang out?

DENNIS

Because you *are* a fuck-up. So am I! So is everyone we *know*. What is the big deal?

WARREN

And how come every time I said I liked a girl you immediately say she's got a fat ass or like has no tits or she's got a horse face or whatever. You know? Jessica Goldman is the first girl I ever had a chance with who was like clearly good-looking enough that you weren't able to make me feel like a second-rate asshole for wanting to go out with her.

DENNIS

You are really making me mad. That's what you're mad about? Because of that time I said that girl Susan had a horse face? That's just the way I talk, man. We all talk that way, it doesn't mean anything. You can't like suddenly turn around and act all fuckin' hurt and sensitive about that shit, that's the way we *are* with each other. Besides, that girl Susan *did* have a horse face, and everybody else could *see* it. I'm just the only one who *says* it. And when you're with a really good-looking girl I fuckin' say *that*. So don't give me this shit from the back *benches* of the fuckin' *peanut* gallery because it's total bullshit, and I am already so *sick* of you after hanging out with you for less than twenty-four hours in a row that I'm like two seconds away from beating the fucking shit out of you, you little fuckin' asshole! (*Pause.*) What do you *mean* I'm not on your *side*?

WARREN

I'm sure you love me, man, and you're totally like my personal hero, but I really don't get the feeling that you are.

A moment. DENNIS *steps back. His face twists into a strange shape and then he breaks out with a surprising choking sob. He starts crying. This goes on for a moment.* WARREN *watches him coldly.*

WARREN

What are you crying about?

DENNIS

What do you *think* I'm crying about?!

WARREN

I assume you feel bad about something you think has happened to you.

DENNIS

No . . . It's because you said I was your hero.

WARREN

Oh.

DENNIS *goes to the kitchenette and blows his nose with a paper towel. Pause.*

DENNIS

So what are you saying? You want to like, stop being friends with me?

WARREN

I don't know, man. I'm not like, breaking *up* with you . . . I'm not your *girl*friend.

DENNIS

So what are you saying?

> WARREN

I don't know.

Silence.

> DENNIS

Well . . . I can't really . . .

Silence.

> WARREN

Let's just drop it.

> DENNIS

All right.

Silence.

> WARREN

Can I have that money?

DENNIS *gives* WARREN *the nine hundred dollars.*

> WARREN

Well . . . I'm only eighteen hundred short.

> DENNIS

Well—I'll start moving what's left of this shit today and see how much we can scrape up.

> WARREN

It doesn't matter.

Silence.

> DENNIS

You wanna smoke pot?

> WARREN

All right.

DENNIS *goes to his bedside table and takes out a small plastic bag of pot.*

WARREN

Where did you get that?

DENNIS

I got it from Stuey last night. Christian sold him some. I'd still like to find out where Christian got it. It fuckin' pisses me off that these ragamuffins are like running around copping drugs that I don't know about. I was gonna get some of that heroin from Stuey till it killed him. I hope it's understood in the community that this coke is really good and that Stuey just overdid it.

WARREN

I'm sure it is.

DENNIS *starts rolling a joint.*

WARREN

It is sort of amazing that one of us actually died. You know? (*Pause.*) Like my Dad is always saying, "Do you know how *bad* you guys would have to fuck up before anything really serious ever happened to you? You and all your friends who went to that fuckin' school where they think it's gonna cripple you for *life* if they teach you how to *spell*? (*Pause.*) Do you know what happens to other kids who do the kind of shit you guys do? They *die*, man. And the only difference between you and them is my money . . . (*Pause.*) But the fact is, he's just so freaked out of his mind that he did so well, and it all blew up in his face anyway . . . Like he did this great enterprising thing for himself and his family, and made a fortune in this incredibly tough racket, and got a house on the park without any help from anyone, and he never felt bad for anyone who couldn't do the same thing. But when he was at the height of his powers, he totally lost control of his own daughter, and she ended up getting beaten to death by some guy from the world next door to us. And there was nothing he could do about it. (*Pause.*) So . . . for the last nine years he's been trying to literally *pound* his life back into shape. But it's not really going too well, because he's totally by himself. (*Pause.*) You know?

DENNIS

I guess. (*Pause.*) I can't *believe* you don't think I'm on your *side*.

Pause. WARREN *looks at him as if from a very great distance.*

WARREN

All right, all right. You're on my side.

DENNIS *lights up.*

DENNIS

So? What are you gonna do?

WARREN

I don't know, man. I guess I'll just go home.

DENNIS *smokes pot.* WARREN *sits there.*

The lights fade out.